D0579972

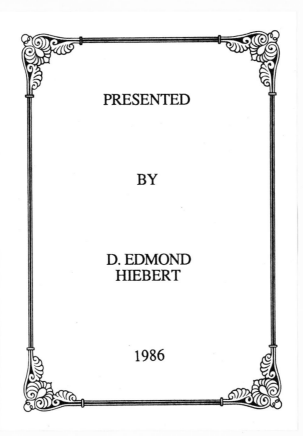

PRESENTED

BY

D. EDMOND
HIEBERT

1986

To Conquer
Loneliness

BV
4911
.W3

To Conquer Loneliness

Harold Blake Walker

Harper & Row, Publishers

New York

HIEBERT LIBRARY
Fresno Pacific College—M.B. Seminary
WITHDRAWN
Fresno, Calif. 93702

26826

TO CONQUER LONELINESS. *Copyright © 1966 by Harold B. Walker. Printed in the United States of America. All rights reserved. No part of this book may be used or reproduced in any manner whatsoever without written permission except in the case of brief quotations embodied in critical articles and reviews. For information address Harper & Row, Publishers, Incorporated, 49 East 33rd Street, New York, N.Y. 10016.*

LIBRARY OF CONGRESS CATALOG CARD NUMBER: 66-15047

C-R

Contents

Introduction   vii

1 – LONELY LANDSCAPE   1

2 – LONELY INSCAPE   18

3 – WE ALL NEED EACH OTHER   34

4 – STRANGE ESTRANGEMENT   51

5 – COUNTDOWN ALONE   67

6 – GUILTY OUTSIDER   82

7 – I'M SORRY FOR ME   99

8 – ISOLATED BY ILLNESS   116

9 – GIVE ME YOUR TEARS   132

10 – CREATIVE SOLITUDE   145

Notes   161

Index   169

Introduction

The day is sodden, dreary, dark, and dripping, with the clouds hung low over the valley and the mountain peaks hidden. The usually pert hummingbirds are drooping in the branches of a pine tree outside my window. Even the normally spirited little chickadees have retreated into themselves and given up their quest for juicy bugs and ants. The blue jays, whose graceful hopping from limb to limb is a joy to watch, are listless. It is a day that invites loneliness and brooding.

There are many such days when the human spirit droops in keeping with the weather. The world outside seems ominous and unfriendly, as if testing the resilience of man and bird and beast. Depression is in the air and heaviness in the spirit. The mind is dull, reflecting the dullness of sky, dark with black and gray. Nothing seems to lift the heart, to inspire gaiety or mirth.

Sodden, dreary days, of course, do not last forever. They are, however, a symbol of the moods of life. Times of depression and wearisome aloneness fall upon us all. They break in upon us unexpectedly, turning joy into the sadness of self-pity and laughter into tears. All of the unhappy memories and disappointments, hurts and failures of the past suddenly overwhelm us. We are haunted by all the miseries of yesterday and the day before. We feel alone, without sunlight or hope.

Emily Dickinson caught a common human mood in her lines,

> The Sky is low—the Clouds are mean.
> A Travelling Flake of Snow
> Across a Barn or Through a Rut
> Debates if it will go—

A Narrow Wind complains all Day
How someone treated him
Nature, like Us is sometimes caught
Without her Diadem.[1]

We often are caught bereft of the diadem of hope and we feel terribly alone under a brooding sky. Even companionship does not lift us. We are alienated from all the sources of meaning and value, buried in ourselves, swamped by our egocentric predicament.

There are many things that contribute to our feelings of depressed loneliness: the landscape around us that seems unfriendly; an immature "inscape," preoccupied with the self; illness; unhappy marriage; difficult decisions; the loss by death of those we have loved. It may be that we never can escape from the essential aloneness of the self, different from any other self, and necessarily grappling alone with the deepest issues of life. There is a lonesome valley through which each of us must travel by ourselves.

If we cannot escape periods of loneliness there are, nevertheless, resources of mind and spirit able to take us through valleys and shadows to the sunlight on the other side. There are possibilities of fellowship to be explored, spiritual insights to be won, and intellectual companionships to be discovered. We can move beyond loneliness to the creativity of solitude.

This book is for lonely men and women who have lost contact with the sources of meaning for life. It is for those who feel they are walking alone in "a fellowless firmament," haunted by days and nights of isolation from friendship and love.

In writing this book I am deeply indebted to my wife, Mary Alice, for her constant encouragement, diligent research, inspiring companionship, and helpful suggestions; to my secretary, Mrs. Thomas Morrison, for her careful preparation of the manuscript, and to the congregation of the First Presbyterian Church of Evanston, whose affection and loyalty are a source of strength and satisfaction.

HAROLD BLAKE WALKER

Evanston, Illinois
January 4, 1966

*To Conquer
Loneliness*

1

Lonely Landscape

A THOUGHTFUL PHYSICIAN who takes time to deal with his patients as whole persons says he has discovered that "Ninety-nine out of a hundred individuals are lonely. The one who says he isn't probably is." The doctor's judgment is accurate, and it requires very little research on the Main Streets of the United States to validate the fact that loneliness is stamped on America's face and etched deeply into its heart.

Anyone who counsels men and women today can document the lonely face of the United States with endless case studies. After I had given an address to a women's club, a middle-aged woman came forward with several others. In the course of the conversation she said, "You never will know how lonely I am." Immediately the others nodded in agreement and one of them remarked, "I guess that goes for all of us."

The popular song of a few years ago, "All Alone," sounded the note of yearning for fellowship, and Amy Lowell in her poem "The Day That Was That Day" captured the same mood in the words of an isolated farm woman:

> My ears is achin' to hear words,
> Words like what's written in books,
> Words that would make me all bright like a spring day.[1]

We all ache for words in which "deep calls to deep," in which we find each other in rich and rewarding communion. But we are "like ships that pass in the night," and while we speak in passing our speaking seldom penetrates beneath the surface. Ego brushes against ego but there is too little genuine communication.

1

DISCONNECTEDNESS

Basically we appear to be disconnected from the centers of meaning and value, with each of us in a separate sphere and without adequate bridges between us. The portrait in its extremest form is to be found in Karl Olson's book *Passion,* in which he pictures a vagrant, an elderly derelict, drifting across a run-down street. The man was "dirty, bearded, ragged and befogged." His feet were stuck into old brogans without laces and he shuffled along unconscious of the melancholy appearance he offered to the world.

There was nobody to care whether the drifter lived or died, no one to say in the morning, "Joe, it's time to get up. Take your bath and shave while I'm getting breakfast." There was no one to say, "Joe, your shoes need laces; here's a pair," or to say, "Good-by, have a good day." Nobody tried to make Joe respectable. He was altogether outside the pale of respectable fellowship. He knew only one world, the world inside the bottle, and he shuffled in search of a drink as fast as his flapping shoes would move him.

Nowhere could one find a more devastating portrait of human isolation and lostness. Alone in himself, cut off from all communion and fellowship, the vagrant's existence was devoid of all we call "life." Life hinges on relationships between man and man, and man and God. It depends on a sense of community and connectedness.

Unhappily, we live in a fragmented culture. The truth is suggested by three simple illustrations taken from contemporary life. The first is the comment of a middle-aged industrial worker, who spends his days winding copper wire for electric motors. He earns a good wage, owns his own home, and has a family, his wife and two children. He is not unhappy about his earnings; on the contrary, he has done rather well and has saved a little money. But he feels frustrated. Why? He explained his feelings by saying, "I've been working for the company for ten years, doing the same thing day after day. Nobody ever has explained to me why what I am doing is important or what relationship it has to the total business. I've never met any of the brass who make the decisions around here." Then he added, "The trouble is we aren't connected up to anything."

The second illustration is a conversation I overheard between two young women in a restaurant. They sat at a table next to the one where I was eating my lunch. They ordered Scotch and soda and proceeded to tell the world in general the nature of their troubles. Their landlady, they agreed, was, as they put it, "a stinker." The lady who lived in the apartment above them was impossible: she moved furniture half the night. The two young women had no use for the supervisor where they worked and when they had finished polishing her off there wasn't much left. Then they began talking about their plans for the weekend. They were really going out on the town. One of them said, "We might as well get some fun out of life." Obviously, the two young women were disconnected, without any relationship to the sources of meaning and value in life. They were "unattached as tumbleweeds."

The third illustration was suggested by a scene in a television show some time ago. A family sat down to dinner and a teen-age girl tried several times to begin a conversation touching on her need for understanding and guidance. But each time she began to speak somebody interrupted with, "Please pass the beans," or "Pass the salt," until finally she retreated into herself in pained aloneness. The preoccupied egos of those around the table dried up the streams of communication.

It is such existential situations that led Jean-Paul Sartre to insist that we are isolated from others, from past and future, from meaning and value. We can count on nobody but ourselves because we are alone, abandoned on earth, and without help. Life is absurd and love is impossible. So, Sartre goes on, we are condemned to futility in an impersonal world and in a universe with neither heart nor meaning. His pessimism is bleak and there is "no exit" from it.

MECHANICAL VOICES

The pessimism of Jean-Paul Sartre is partly a product of his own past and partly of a cultural climate shot through with technology and automation, a society that is increasingly dominated by machines and material values. We have been overtaken by a mass culture that has transformed every aspect of our lives. Parents used to wonder how they spent their time before they had children. Today we ask ourselves, "What did we do with our time before television?"

As a nation we now devote more time to mass-produced communications than to paid work, or play, or anything except sleep. Television alone of the mass media consumes one-fifth of the average individual's waking life. Our minds are cluttered with the clatter of radio while we drive on the highways, and personal communication is blotted out by the mechanical voices that fill the air waves.

Mass culture isolates man from society. We develop loyalties to brand names and TV programs, but we feel very little kinship to the nameless and faceless thousands who make our way of life possible. We are what Thorstein Veblen called "conspicuous consumers" of the products of our automated society, but we are underprivileged in our interpersonal relationships. We understand the lament of the "Ancient Mariner" who complained,

> Alone, alone, all, all alone,
> Alone on a wide, wide sea!
> And never a saint took pity on
> My soul in agony.[2]

Aldous Huxley describes our time as the era of "Fordism," a philosophy which demands that we sacrifice the man to the machine and the mass. People become things, and persons become merely productive symbols with deadly effect on the creative arts, the humanities, and the dignity of men. We gear our lives to business organizations or to machines, and our relationships are largely as thing to thing. We are insiders in the sense that we are instruments of production and distribution, but we are outsiders when it comes to the personal relationships which stimulate communication and creative thinking. We are in the organization, but we feel isolated and alone in it.

"I live alone," said a middle-aged woman, "and all day I work at an IBM machine until I feel as if I could scream. I can't talk to a machine," she went on, "and at night I can't talk to my TV set. It keeps talking at me." She wanted rapport with someone who would talk with her about books and poetry, religion and life. She wished she could communicate her feelings about life and the world to somebody who would understand and respond. In short, she wanted to be "connected up" to some responsive source of meaning.

Modern technology has leveled our lives to a thin, horizontal plane of materialism. We are homogenized as a bottle of milk, but most of the butterfat has been removed. The vertical dimension has vanished in our quest for things and conveniences. Indeed, we are lost in a forest so cluttered with things that we can no longer see the stars. We see blinking neon signs instead. Unhappily, our materialism has left us with a crop of alcoholism, divorce, mental disorders, boredom, and loneliness.

Even education is suffering from the depersonalizing effects of technology. College examinations used to be trying experiences, endeavoring to test the knowledge of such matters as the European roots of American nineteenth-century transcendentalism or the impact of Immanuel Kant on philosophy. And, of course, professors spent endless hours correcting examinations and groaning inwardly at how little of the subject matter got through to their students. But at least there was a personal relationship between professor and student. Each knew the other by name.

Machines have changed all that, and college tests have become multiple choice affairs in which the student blackens one of a series of numbers corresponding to the choices offered, a device which permits the examination to be graded swiftly and mechanically. Under such conditions a professor can give a test to a class of three hundred to five hundred nameless students about whom he knows nothing. So, there is little that can be called vital communication between teacher and student in modern college classrooms. One college student said sadly, "I'm not even a name. I'm a number."

Increasingly we are set in a world of things and machines in which totals, aggregates, and masses count for more and more, and individuals are lost sight of. Contemporary society is the social equivalent of nature in Tennyson's words:

> So careful of the type she seems,
> So careless of the single life.[3]

The technological society which is changing the inner as well as the outer aspects of life with television, syndicated news, and what is worse, syndicated opinion, has created a standardized mind, which seriously threatens the capacity of individuals to communicate creatively. Conversation seldom plumbs the depths, and our relationships are so superficial that our sense of aloneness is intensified.

DISPLACED PERSONS

It is not only the technological revolution that has left us with a sense of disconnected loneliness, but also the fact that we are a nation of displaced persons, uprooted and on wheels. The woman uprooted from her home town, Kansas City, and planted in Chicago because her husband was transferred to the Windy City, spoke for multitudes. "I hate Chicago," she said. "All my friends are in Kansas City." So far as she could see, there was nothing and nobody in Chicago. Mentally she still was living in her beloved home town.

Physical aloneness, being separated from those we love and care about, is an experience common to the company wife who follows her husband from city to city while he pushes toward the top of the business ladder. He manages the successive changes with reasonable facility because he is involved in business with associates who share his toil. She feels isolated and alone, friendless in an unfriendly world. The people and the places she loves are elsewhere and the new people she meets cannot take the place of those she has left.

Walter Prescott Webb, who has studied the effect of life on the frontier on American character, points out that in the days of the westward drive "loneliness" was used to describe a psychological condition. Quoting from a Kansas plainsman, he says in his book *The Great Plains,*

Did you ever hear of "loneliness" as a fatal disease? Once, back in the days when father and I were bringing up long-legged sheep from Mexico, we picked up a man near Las Vegas who had lost his way. He was in a terrible state. It wasn't the result of being lost. He had "loneliness." Born on the plains you get accustomed to them; but on people not born there the plains sometimes have an appalling effect. "He's got loneliness," we would say of such a man.[4]

So there are in our day multitudes of men and women of whom it can be said, "they've got loneliness."

You and I have known the experience of being uprooted, put down in an unfamiliar environment, tortured by self-doubt, wondering if we are able to make a new life in new surroundings. We have felt as if we were on an island in an alien sea, without boat or paddle to get to the mainland where there are people and friendship and affection. If only we could get to the mainland and beyond our aloneness.

Stranded in New York City because my plane from Chicago was late and I had missed a train for Buck Hill Falls, Pennsylvania, I took a walk one evening, strolling along Broadway to pass the time. It was a gloomy night with fog rolling in from the ocean, but the lights were bright and thousands of men and women crowded the sidewalks. Tin-pan music issued from basement bars. A man was selling what were alleged to be jumping dolls. He was doing a brisk business until somebody discovered that the dolls were attached to a black thread, which two men, leaning against a nearby building, manipulated skillfully to keep the dolls jumping. A drunk lurched and swayed along the street, greeting strangers with profuse enthusiasm. Women wearing mink and well-dressed men waited in theater entrances here and there.

There on the crowded street I felt frightfully alone and without roots. There was no one to speak to; no one to care in the least how I felt. Nobody stopped to say "Hello! How are you?" except the drunk who was too cordial and incoherent to be helpful. Two young men, wearing black leather jackets, pushed their way through the crowd, deliberately bumping into people to express their hostility to something or to somebody. I suspected there were multitudes of anonymous people on the street that night as lonesome and lost as I. We were all lost, isolated in our aloneness.

The poignant sense of isolation which I felt on a New York street is akin to the aloneness uprooted families feel in new and unfamiliar surroundings. "They've got loneliness," and it seems to grow worse with each new move from city to city and neighborhood to neighborhood. What is the use of cultivating friends and interests in new places when we soon will be pulling up stakes and starting for somewhere else? We may as well make the best of what we cannot help and learn to live with our uprootedness.

Migrant families, moving from place to place, soon discover that the children are hurting inside, feeling insecure and lonely. Edna St. Vincent Millay, in a penetrating poem, suggested the feeling of infants trying to find the warmth of security in a strange new world. She wrote:

Intense and terrible, I think, must be the loneliness
Of infants—look at all
The Teddy-bears clasped in slumber in slatted cribs
Painted pale-blue or pink.
And all the Easter Bunnies, dirty and disreputable, that deface
The white pillow and the sterile, immaculate, sunny, turning
pleasantly into space,
Dainty abode of Baby—try to replace them
With new ones, come Easter again, fluffy and white, and with
a different smell;
Release with gentle force from the horrified embrace,
That hugs until the stitches give and the stuffing shows,
His only link with a life of his own, the only thing he really knows . . .
Try to sneak it out of sight.
If you wish to hear anger yell glorious
From air-filled lungs through a throat unthrottled
By what the neighbours will say;
If you wish to witness a human countenance contorted
And convulsed and crumpled by helpless grief and despair,
Then stand beside the slatted crib and say, "There, there," and
take the toy away.[5]

The loneliness of children, beset by nameless fears, is intensified by our migrant ways. Once when we moved from New York to Oklahoma City one of our sons developed a nameless pain and refused to get out of bed to go to school. Three doctors examined him and found nothing wrong. We finally insisted that he go back to school. Twenty years later we found out what was wrong. His older brother had been ill at school one day and his mother called at the school to take him home. The younger boy saw his mother and his brother leaving and was quite sure we were moving again and leaving him behind. So, he took to his bed just to make sure we would not take off without him.

Even the warmth and love which surrounded our son in the family could not entirely compensate for the uprootedness from a familiar place among friends and neighbors. There was a sense of security in the home he had left. He could ride his tricycle down the block and visit with people he knew. He could play with children he called his friends, and he could find his way back to the security of the home he had known since birth. He was somebody, too, because his neighbors knew his name and where he lived. But he was nameless and an outsider in the new neighborhood. He did not yet belong to the group in his new environment. So, he was hurting inside, insecure, and more than a little afraid.

To be sure, adults are more mature than children, or at least they should be. They do not fear being left behind when business dictates a change. But they share something of the feeling of a child, the sense of not belonging, of being "out of things." They feel "nameless" because nobody knows them, and they walk the streets without meeting anyone who calls them by name. Often they get the disease called "loneliness."

THE STRANGER

Another aspect of the landscape surrounding us complicates our adjustment to new places: a common suspicion of strangers. More than a generation ago Rudyard Kipling wrote "The Stranger," a poem which included this verse:

> The Stranger within my gates,
> He may be evil or good,

But I cannot tell what powers control—
What reasons sway his mood;
Nor when the Gods of his far off land
Shall repossess his blood.[6]

The stranger is a stranger and we do not know "what powers control" his thinking or behavior.

Mary McDermott Shideler, a minister's wife, described her experience in a new community. She was, she says, "a threat to the people in our congregation" because they were unable to predict what she might think or do. They were quite unable to discern what inner motives or intentions might direct her behavior. Her preference for knitting socks rather than embroidering clothespin bags seemed peculiar to the other women. While she admired their families and their handiwork, she praised the right things for the wrong reasons, or the wrong things for the right reasons. "Being incalculable," Mrs. Shideler wrote, "I was dangerous, and nothing I said or did could obliterate the peril."[7]

The stranger always is something of a threat. We welcome him, or her, with some reservations. The new employee in a business office constitutes a danger to those already there. He upsets the balance. If he is too competent, he is a peril to mediocrity already there. If he is incompetent, he is a source of annoyance. In one way or another people have to adjust themselves to the stranger they cannot avoid. He is a nuisance and an irritation and, quite possibly, he will disrupt the *status quo*. We rather wish he would go home, and he, feeling like an outsider, wishes he were somewhere else.

If we are the strangers, we may decide we never will be able to break into the inner circle of the community or the business. We may become discouraged and move elsewhere. On the other hand, we may persist, hang on, trying to overcome the barriers that separate us from the "old-timers" who have their little clique. Possibly we may be accepted, taken in, by those who determine social relationships in the community.

A young man, a graduate of the Harvard Business School, went to work for an old established firm. He was full of ideas and visions of what could be done to modernize the business and increase its profits. But he was a stranger and a threat, and the employees and the managers shunted him here and there to avoid changes he proposed. He may have been overzealous, undiplomatic at times, but he was so completely boxed out that finally he left the firm. Later, in another business, he made rapid progress as a highly valued idea man.

There are times when as strangers we persist, hang on, and try to break into the fellowship of those who seem resolved to keep us outside. Possibly a business move puts the family down into a new community where the lines of social life are solidly drawn. The stranger is not welcome. She may be a graduate of Vassar or Smith, competent and brilliant, but her qualifications do not automatically admit her into the sanctum of the social elite. She may seem to be a threat to those who exercise power and influence.

"They just won't accept me," said an attractive young woman in her mid-thirties. "They seem to think I have the measles or halitosis." Those in the neighborhood were polite and courteous, but they already had their bridge clubs and their social groups, and strangers were not included. If, in time, someone moved away or died, the outsider might become an insider. But there would be a long wait until the possessors of social power decided the stranger would be no threat to themselves.

One thoughtful woman, invited to be a member of an exclusive group after some twelve years in a community remarked, "Well, I finally made it." But the years on the outside looking in were lonely ones, often hard to take. Unhappily, the strangers on the outside looking in are legion in our uprooted culture and the pain occasioned by human exclusiveness is a heavy burden for multitudes of men and women.

Curiously enough, the stranger who finally becomes the insider soon forgets the painful experience of exclusion. He, or she, becomes one of the excluders, part of the power structure intent on protecting itself. New strangers suffer and feel the pangs of loneliness. The process goes on as if the insiders did not know that from the perspective of all the great religions, rejection of the stranger is a sin.

IN THE MIDST OF CROWDS

Paradoxically, there is still another characteristic of our contemporary culture that increases our sense of lonely disconnectedness, namely, the population explosion. With people, people everywhere, one would think we would be less lonely than our forebears. But it is not so, because the crowd is lonely. Curiously, the larger the crowd, the more disconnected we are in it. The truth is suggested in the musical version of *Street Scene,* produced in 1947 with music by Kurt Weill and lyrics by Langston Hughes. In the musical Sam sings "Lonely House," in which he complains, "Lonely house, lonely me, funny with so many neighbors how lonely it can be."

Unhappily, proximity does not guarantee a sense of community. We may be together in physical space and at the same time isolated in the sense that we are unable to communicate with those around us. A foreigner who had spent many months in this country observed: "Americans visit so many parties and search for so many opportunities to be with people that they do not even become aware of how lonely they are. They only escape into company."[8] The company does not satisfy. Somehow we do not feel at home. We are strangers in crowds, unable to find the right words to open doors of communion and communication. Charles Lamb spoke for us all when he wrote, "Cannot the heart in the midst of crowds feel frightfully alone."

Our contemporary culture has intensified the feeling of Charles Lamb. The books that have been popular in the postwar United States reflect our plight. *The Lonely Crowd, The Organization Man,* or Salinger's fiction are meaningful because they find us where we are. The books have one major theme, the overwhelming and oppressive system, the pressure of the crowd, and how on earth do I escape from it to be myself and to share somehow, somewhere, the values that make life worth living?

Remi Nadeau's book called *California: The New Society,* is a study of people's private lives. It is a portrait of "a society of the unassociated." It is not that Californians are deficient in "togetherness." They have achieved, says Mr. Nadeau, "super-togetherness." They are in each other's swimming pools much of the time. But he finds their "togetherness" does not produce community. Except for their newspapers they have no means of communicating, and communication makes community. Their togetherness is escapism, not shared responsibility.

There is in California, Mr. Nadeau notes, a magnificent freedom in which people have time and opportunity to turn their backs on each other's difficulties. As with people all over our land, life is mostly a matter of virtuous materialism, of getting "established in the world," but without any sense of connectedness to the real centers of meaning and value in personal relationships.

Often I have thought how much easier it must have been for my grandfather to love his neighbors than for me to love mine. When he settled in Denver, his was the only house within a radius of two miles. He could visit his neighbors when he felt like it. On the way to his office behind his team of grays, he met little or no traffic. We know how different it is now. Certainly it is no easy task to love our neighbors when we are caught in the rush-hour traffic jam.

Isolated in our mechanical conveyances we see our neighbors as obstacles to our progress. Too many people in too many automobiles constitute a problem even for those who are disposed to be neighborly. Crowded trains and buses, elevators and streets try our patience with impersonal pressure and we find ourselves developing feelings of hostility. A crowded world, far from creating community, increases conflict and feelings of disconnectedness.

THE ISOLATION OF MEANING

Our sense of aloneness has been accentuated, too, by the fact that "the faith of our fathers" is not exactly "living still." On the contrary, it is under steady and unrelenting attack. Archibald MacLeish said in an Evanston lecture that his father was a man of confident faith, a faith supported by the consensus of the community. The old gentleman was certain that when his back was against the wall there was something solid on which to lean for strength and support. Mr. MacLeish added that in our time there is no such "consensus of faith." We do not trust in the values of the past and in "the faith of our fathers" as sources of strength to hold us steady when we are under stress.

There was a note of wistfulness in the reminiscences of Mr. MacLeish, and the same yearning appears now and then in Walter Lippmann, who writes of our "spiritual uneasiness." The malady is caused, he believes, by the "impact of science upon religious certainty and of technological progress upon the settled order of family, class and community." We seem to be homeless, unsettled, and unled, and as a consequence we are haunted by anxiety and loneliness.

Our disconnected isolation from centers of meaning and value rooted in "the faith of our fathers" is illustrated by contemporary novelists, most of whom assume a philosophical pose which leaves their characters isolated in an impersonal cosmos which is in itself without meaning. Viktor Frankl, a Viennese psychiatrist, insists that the great neurosis of our time is the failure of modern man to find meaning in his existence.

John Ciardi, a *Saturday Review* critic, once shared a Religious Week panel at a New Jersey college where he developed the naturalist thesis. He spoke by request on the theme, "The Images of Man in Literature." He described the universe as such naturalistic writers as Zola, Hardy, Norman Mailer, James Jones, and others saw it. It was a vast and indifferent universe, devoid of spiritual or moral values, only a physical organism of basic unconcern for man and his works. When he sat down, one of his fellow panelists spread his arms and asked, "Whence cometh my help?" Perhaps the deeper question was, "Whence cometh my meaning and worth?"

Sometimes when I read the novels of Tennessee Williams, Norman Mailer, William Faulkner, James Jones, and their kind, I have the feeling that their portraits of life's degradation have been carried to a point at which their stories lose contact with reality. Some critics insist, to be sure, that the novelists are searching for meaning in life, and their characters are disreputable and disgusting because life has neither meaning nor significance. Character unravels because of a fruitless quest for some connection between the self and the universe that suggests meaning in it all.

Norman Cousins suggests thoughtfully that there is a confusion here between cause and effect. "The disintegration," he says, "is the result of a poverty of values and not of a serious but vain search for meaning in life." Obviously, the man who lives in a mood of disconnectedness, who sees no lines between yesterday and tomorrow, who never has found the joy of enlistment in the service of love or truth or beauty, is doomed to a meaningless existence and to wistfulness, loneliness, and anxiety.

ISOLATING FEAR

Obviously, both the outward and the inward stresses of contemporary culture have made us vulnerable to suspicion and fear and so have accentuated our loneliness. The central character in Howard Spring's novel *Fame Is the Spur,* looking at the world of 1940 and thinking back over his long life, comments that the world of 1940 was drastically different from the world in which he grew to maturity. In the world of his youth, "No good had seemed impossible," but in 1940 he began to live in a new age in which "No evil, no bestiality, no treason or treachery seemed incredible."[9]

The word "anxiety" became a cornerstone of our psychology in the 1940's, but we kept hoping against hope that we would be able to recover "the good old days," and return to what President Harding once called "normalcy." Those who know history, however, are aware that the world is back to normal. The abnormal ages have been the times of tranquility and confidence when no good seemed impossible. The world of the first century was normal and so is ours. The problem is to cope with our anxieties in times that are essentially normal.

Our fears have enfeebled and divided us one from another, as Robert Ardrey's play *Sing Me No Lullaby* suggests. The story concerns an American scientist whose loyalty has been erroneously questioned because of political ideas he had when he was in college in the thirties. Of the world nuclear physics has created, Mike says, "The chain reaction they perfected in Chicago didn't work out quite right. What it splits is people, one from another. The fission gives off fear."[10]

Under the stress of our fear there has been a steady erosion of trust and good will. The more delicate human relationships have been splintered by suspicion. We are suspicious of neighbors whose political views do not accurately reflect our own. We are afraid of our own freedom, not quite willing to listen to points of view that run contrary to our own. So, suspicion and mistrust multiply and people are split from one another. We have become isolated in our fears.

Boris Pasternak and others have written concerning the lonely isolation of individuals in Soviet Russia. Nobody quite trusts or believes in his neighbor. K. C. Wu paints the picture of the isolating fear in his fine novel *The Lane of Eternal Stability*. With the coming of the Communists, anxiety led to the splitting of society into a collection of lonely individuals unwilling to communicate with neighbors and friends, fearful lest some thoughtless word lead to trouble with the Party.

Even children are fearful, which can be documented by their choice of heroes, says J. Chapman Bradley. In balmier days, he notes, Donald Duck was their hero. From their places of security they could laugh at poor Donald, badgered by fate, beset by vicissitudes, and always coming up with the short end of the stick. They could laugh at Donald in those days because they felt secure. But the children of today have switched to "The Virginian" or "Gunsmoke's" Matt Dillon, stern yet genial guardians of justice. Mothers say they are having trouble because their children want to go to bed with their cowboy boots on and insist on draping their six-guns on the bedposts, so that they may spring into action at a moment's notice.

Call it fad if you will, I suppose it is. The whole fear psychology of our time is a fad, but it is real and its roots are in the nature of our age and in the way we look at it. The Pallid Giant of fear walks abroad and howls down the chimneys of even the most rugged of individualists. So we divide against each other, liberals against conservatives, the right against the left, the Party of Innovation against the Party of Memory, and vice versa.

The landscape that is the backdrop for our lives is not likely to change decisively for the better in the years to come. Technology, automation, and the population explosion are here to stay. We will go on as individuals and families migrating from place to place, and there will continue to be those who scorn "the faith of our fathers" as a valid source of strength for days of confusion and strain. If the landscape is forbidding, deepening our sense of aloneness, our hope is in what someone called "the inscape," in the interior resources of our minds and hearts.

Are we to become helpless victims of the external forces that impinge upon our lives, or are we able to fashion images of ourselves worthy to cope with our tomorrows and build bridges to take us beyond loneliness?

Lonely Inscape

M OST OF what we call ourselves we cannot see in a mirror. We perceive physical shape and form, and the image we see in the glass is a portion of ourselves. It reveals something of what we are inside, but most of what Christopher Morley called "the inscape" is hidden from view. What we see in a mirror is what the world sees and identifies with a name. But there is an infinite realm of the unseen and unseeable in us all. There are thoughts and feelings, memories and hopes which hide beneath the skin. There are those areas of the self which Robert Frost described as "desert places" where loneliness centers.

In his perceptive way, Frost described "snow falling and night falling fast," and as he drove through the countryside he could see only a "few weeds and stubble showing" above the white of the snow. Animals, he knew, were "smothered in their lairs." He added,

> I am too absent-spirited to count:
> The loneliness includes me unawares.
>
> And lonely as it is, that loneliness
> Will be more lonely ere it will be less,
>
> . . . .
> I have it in me so much nearer home
> To scare myself with my own desert places.[1]

The landscape seems more lonely than it really is when we scare ourselves with "desert places" nearer home. When the inscape is dreary, without resources of its own, our "desert places" are unrelieved by oases where trees grow and flowers bloom. "I live alone—live is not the exact word," a woman wrote. "I exist alone." She insisted that a single woman without a man for company is "nobody." I thought of the comment of a widow pursued by a number of men whose intentions were something less than the best. She said thoughtfully, "There are some things worse than loneliness." Happily, she had found interior resources to water her "desert places" and she still found her life rewarding and meaningful.

THE ALIVE MIND

Even though the landscape is lonely, the essential source of our aloneness is inside, not outside. There are those who dwell "in a fellowless firmament" and yet are in great company. Their minds are their resource. Milton and Shakespeare are there, along with Wordsworth and Keats and a host of other worthy spirits. They find a strange refreshment in their solitariness.

Edward Dyer sensed the significance of the inscape when he wrote his vital lines,

> My mind to me a kingdom is:
> Such present joys therein I find,
> That it excels all other bliss
> That earth affords.[2]

The wealth of our minds is an endless resource, an asset of boundless scope as many prisoners of the world's tyranny have discovered. An Hungarian physician, now in Budapest, who spent three years in Siberia as a prisoner of the Soviet remarked humbly that two things saved him: his faith in God and the resources of his mind. "Through the years," he said, "I had committed the Scriptures to memory and poetry was my hobby." So, even in isolation from those he loved he was able to avoid the destructiveness of separation from his home and friends. His mind was a kingdom wherein he found joy even in Siberia.

The empty mind turns inward and is bounded by the self. It is haunted by remembered hurts and anxious fears, swamped in the end by towering waves of self-pity. Its inscape is bleak and its horizons zero. The full mind turns outward to embrace the things of beauty that are a joy forever. It brings to its prison cell or rooming house something of the wisdom of Socrates and lifting hints of insight from the prophets and teachers of yesterday. When the self threatens and inward pity tries to overwhelm the man whose mind is rich in knowledge, he never is at a loss to find an antidote.

Most of those whose minds have been creative have known the need for solitude. Thomas Edison, whose deafness shut him from communication with his fellows, found his mind alive in the silence. He needed his aloneness for thinking, for wresting from his intellect the secret of the incandescent light. The flashing tempo of his thought left him no time for loneliness or for the torture of self-pity. There were endless problems to be solved, a thousand experiments to be tried, new vistas of science to be explored.

We cannot run away from loneliness. We take our inscape with us wherever we go. There are those who travel far by ship or plane, haunting the bars of ships and the beer-halls of the continent. They come home no less obsessed by their aloneness than when they left their homes. They see the world, and yet their minds still focus on themselves. If they see the Parthenon, they do not seek to know how Phidias carved and Pericles ruled. They come away with no memories of Plato and the grandeur of his thought and they do not ask of the decline of the Golden Age of Athens.

Recently in visiting with a man who is trying to find ways to stimulate the minds and enrich the characters of young people we fell to talking about loneliness. "I suppose all of us have moments of loneliness," he said. "It is not a problem for me, however, because my mind is constantly wrestling with ideas." He noted that when he traveled, he studied the activities and the behavior of young people, always trying to discover "what makes them tick." He added significantly, "When I travel, I always have a purpose."

I was reminded of that conversation on board a ship crossing the Atlantic. On board were many lonely men and women just trying to get through from Monday to Sunday. I was on my way with my wife to travel through Turkey and Greece following "in the footsteps of St. Paul." We were eagerly anticipating our adventure, having followed the Great Apostle in imagination for many years and aware of the message he preached. One woman remarked thoughtfully as we talked: "I am sure travel is helpful only when one has a mission, otherwise it does little to stimulate the mind."

The mind alive is a necessary ingredient in the conquest of loneliness. A wise young widow observed that after her husband died, the days seemed endless and empty. "I knew," she said, "I had no choice but to put my mind to work. So, I began to study French. I kept vocabulary cards all over the apartment and whenever I began to be sorry for myself I began to learn new words or turned on the record player to listen for correct pronunciation." She hopes some day to be able to teach French. Happily, her venture in renewed learning has been a benediction. She has moved beyond self-pity to self-fulfillment.

Martha Ingram, the central character in *Knights and Dragons* by Elizabeth Spencer, struggled through the lonely days of isolation from her husband, divorce, and misery. She sought freedom from her aloneness in an affair with another man and finally achieved control over herself, though at high cost. Miss Spencer wrote of her,

She more and more arranged to do things alone, a curious tendency, for loneliness once had been a torment, whereas now she regarded almost everything her eyes fell upon with an equal sense of companionship; her compatibility was with the world . . . she was a friend now to any landscape, a companion to cloud and sky.[3]

Martha cultivated her mind and her sensitivity to beauty and truth, turning her thoughts outward in such fashion that her intellectual vitality saved her from the agony of aloneness.

We have a choice, you and I. Through the years of growing toward maturity we can make our minds into assets or we can leave them to rust into liabilities. We can invite the lonely inscape, the mental vacuum, or we can so fill our minds with truth and beauty that when we are alone we are not devastated.

One man I know whose deafness is a limitation has a hobby not only of collecting old books but of reading them as well. He is forever quoting some gem from a long forgotten volume. He finds analogies between yesterday and today that stir his imagination. He is vitally alive with what he knows and his mind is an asset that saves him from isolation.

There is a hint of wisdom for us all in the Master's parable of the man possessed by an unclean spirit haunting his life. With strong resolution he swept his mind clear only to suffer the invasion of "seven other spirits" more annoying than the first. He learned what all of us must learn, namely, that we cannot sweep our minds clear of self-pity, fear, anxiety, and loneliness unless we fill the vacuum with ideas and knowledge that crowd out the unwanted and the hurtful.

INTEGRITY OF SPIRIT

The life of the mind determines the inscape, and so does the life and the vitality of the spirit. There are qualities of character, integrity and honor, faith and trust that buttress the spirit against the assaults of isolation. If the landscape seems lonely because we are out of step with the crowd, the inscape may well be peopled by the saints and heroes of history who kept faith with themselves and God despite the scorn of their contemporaries. We may be at odds with our contemporaries in the name of integrity, and yet at one with the ultimate values of life and history.

Without a solid core of character to gird our confidence, the chasm between the inner self and others becomes wider and wider. We put on masks to hide our deepest convictions and feelings, and we seldom remove them. We talk, play bridge, give presents, tease, and engage in games, always guarding, consciously or unconsciously, the hidden self. If the landscape has made warm and rewarding comradeship difficult, the inscape guarantees our essential aloneness. At odds with ourselves, we are separated from our fellow men and from earth and sky as well.

Through the centuries there have been men and women who

endured isolation from the crowd because they were not isolated from the values that gave meaning to their aloneness. When Jesus approached the end of His life His disciples "left him and fled." They were His most intimate friends and colleagues, but they deserted Him under the pressure of their fear. The crowds that had heard the Master "gladly" turned away. Raucous voices shouted, "Crucify him!" and none stood by to lend Him their strength. He stood alone unwilling to betray the truth He had taught. But Jesus was not alone. He was at one with the very ground of His being. He said, "I am not alone, for the Father is with me."[4]

There is something vital and sustaining in the knowledge that in standing right even in isolation from the crowd we are surrounded by "a vast cloud of witnesses" who walked alone and yet were not alone. In a commencement address, William H. Miller of Chicago, sounded a solid note. "If you wind up lonely because you won't go along with the crowd," said Miller, "I extend some sympathy for your present loneliness, but I confess I feel only envy for the exciting life you have before you."[5] Inner integrity of spirit is exciting because it links us to what is deepest in the nature of reality. It gives us something dependable to strive for, something to live for and die for, something ultimately meaningful.

We are lonely, wistful, and afraid when our lives are committed to nothing that challenges us to be. Character that is worthy of self-respect always is the consequence of commitment. As Jesus said, "The gate is narrow and the way is hard that leads to life, and those who find it are few."[6] It is a way that involves doing what we would rather not and not doing what we would rather because we have given ourselves to something ultimately of worth. The "little aims that end with self" are self-defeating; the large aims that end in God are self-fulfilling.

Many a man has learned "how to win friends and influence people" for his own benefit only to discover that he cannot live with himself. He has created his own interior "desert places," using people for his own ends, trying to make them believe he has their own interests at heart only to find he is lonely for sincere friendship, wistful for forthrightness he has forsaken, and afraid his superficiality may come to light. God has been crowded from all the relationships of such a man's life because he is essentially selfish and uncommitted to anything beyond himself. There is nothing overarching his own spirit to provide significance for his striving.

A child playing alone in her back yard offered the ultimate clue to freedom from loneliness. As she played in the sand a neighbor called over the fence: "Where's your mother, Mary?" "Mom's asleep," came the reply. "Well, where is your little brother?" "He is asleep, too." "Aren't you lonesome, playing all by yourself?" "No," Mary anwered, "I like me." The child's insight was profound. If we are able to like ourselves, to respect ourselves, we are able to cope with aloneness. It is the cracks in character, the self-will and selfishness, and our unlovable ways, that make and keep the inscape lonely and isolated from others and from God.

The autobiography of Jean-Paul Sartre is suggestive. It begins with a perusal of the family album. It pictures those who surrounded young Jean-Paul in his childhood as caricature-like phonies encouraging the literary precociousness of an ugly little toad even phonier than they. Sartre, in the end, denounces himself as a phony to the bone. In a paroxysm of self-hatred, Sartre lashes out at everything—heredity, family, culture, and God.

One who reads Sartre's biography is constrained to feel that his existentialism, so devoid of spiritual depth and with scorn for the very idea of God, is primarily the consequence not of rational thought, but of self-hate bottled within him. Hate for himself and for those who nurtured him left him unable to believe that love is anything but phony. Of course, the God who is love is phony too.

The difference between Sartre and Archibald MacLeish is found at this point. MacLeish, surrounded by affection, committed to the abiding values of his heritage and nurtured by love, believes love to be the ultimate clue to reality. If he finds it difficult to accept God in the terms of his father's thought, he has at least moved from negative skepticism to an awareness that there is something of value in the universe to which a man must commit himself no matter what—namely, love as the clue to the ground of his being.

Our faith in God, or lack of it, therefore, is far more psychological than it is a matter of intellectual proof or the absence of it. Belief is undercut by the knowledge of the inscape that we are phonies. Faith and hope are not lost in logic, but by the absence of integrity and the capacity to love. When we are victims of hostilities and animosities we are conditioned to skepticism. God is driven from the scene where conflicts rage inside and where bitterness divides us from each other. To be sure, we prefer to describe our skepticism in terms of our intellectual sophistication. It satisfies our pride to assume we know too much to believe in God.

Obviously we are making ourselves all the time, creating selves we can respect or laying foundations for an intolerable inscape. Minds enriched by truth and beauty are the bequest of the years, and character that is integrated and steadied by commitment is built day by day. A young woman trying to excuse the intolerable, selfish ways of her father-in-law remarked, "He's difficult because he always has been that way." Character does not just happen. It grows with the years. Lonely old men who are cantankerous simply reflect what they always have been.

SELF-ACCEPTANCE

The building of selves we can live with begins with willingness to accept ourselves and to see ourselves honestly as we are. Unhappily, we often are disposed to compensate for our interior inadequacies not by self-acceptance but by vigorous self-affirmation. That is to say, we affirm our own self-sufficiency and masquerade as the master of things. Walt Whitman pictured the mood of self-affirmation in his "Song of Myself" in which he wrote, "I celebrate myself, and sing myself."[7] He painted the portrait of man the heroic, even though the heroism was tinged with despair and the self-sufficiency darkened by ultimate and final death. The self-sufficiency was something of a pose, at odds with the reality of the inscape.

Our assumptions of superiority often are elaborate self-deceptions designed to help us cope with our inadequacies and our loneliness. Unhappily, they work in reverse. In celebrating ourselves we intensify our separation from other people. Our snobbery invites hostility and rejection. What is more, our pretended self-satisfaction separates us from the source of renewal and hope. God becomes an unneeded appendage and our status and external supports become the only ground of our security.

"So far as I am aware God never did anything for me," an arrogantly successful man remarked. "What I've got, I've earned." Self-sufficient and proud, he was a living symbol of the self-made man. But, as someone remarked, "He relieved the Almighty of a terrible responsibility." He possessed everything and yet he had nothing. He owned all the gadgets a material civilization could provide, but he was frustrated and lonely. He was

> Alive but alone, belonging—where?
> Unattached as tumbleweeds.[8]

Man, the self-sufficient, the master of things, is a lonely master, "unattached as tumbleweeds" blowing across the prairie.

The portrait of ourselves as self-sufficient is suggested eloquently in Walt Whitman's poem, "Crossing Brooklyn Ferry," in which he draws the word picture of himself looking over the rail of the ferry watching, he says, "the fine centrifugal spokes of light round the shape of my head in the sunlit water."[9] The halo image of ourselves as "little lower than the angels" is striking and is repeated toward the end of "Song of Myself," in which Whitman wrote, "And nothing, not God, is greater than one's self is."

Our competence to cope with our aloneness is complicated by pretended superiority. Our hope lies in the grace to accept ourselves and to confess our need to grow in character and wisdom. Despite heroics and stubborn toil, and despite status and wealth, the self-sufficient are aware that the inscape is a shambles of conflict and loneliness. It is not easy to face reality and to accept the fact of need for inner overhauling. And yet, there is no other way to begin fashioning a full mind and a character worthy of honest self-respect.

The cry of the tax collector in the Master's parable needs to be echoed in a multitude of lives, "God be merciful to me, a sinner."[10] Having deceived ourselves with assumptions of superiority and found that the inscape is dry as dust, separated from the source of meaning and value, we have no choice but to accept ourselves the way we are and begin the process of inward renewal, building on foundations of faith and commitment. An athlete, an outstanding star, proud of his powers, popular beyond the dreams of most, suddenly became aware of the superficiality of his life and the transient nature of his status, faced himself and confessed his need for more than applause could offer. "When I finally admitted my own inadequacy and accepted my need for God and for a lot of personal overhauling I found what St. Paul called 'newness of life,' " he said. "Life is richer for me than it ever has been before."

Applause, popularity, and status do not satisfy the demands of the inscape. They are outward props which leave us dependent on externals and do not touch the deeper needs within. They give us a false sense of superiority which the inscape denies when we come to terms with it. Indeed, I have known more than one man, popular, possessing both wealth and status, and yet decisively wistful, lonely, and afraid, unwilling nevertheless to accept his need for God and for spiritual and moral overhauling.

SELF-RESPECT

Our social, interpersonal relationships inevitably hinge on our own self-respect and spiritual security. If the inscape is tortured by conflict, the landscape of people is inescapably alien. If we are unable to respect ourselves we cannot accept with grace and warmth even the adulation of our fellows. There is an inner wall of separation that keeps us from rewarding comradeship. If we are unable to accept ourselves we cannot believe we are accepted by others.

It is the inwardly dissatisfied who fill the taverns on the streets of a thousand cities and towns. "I go to the tavern and drink a few beers in the evening just to get away from myself," said a widow in her forties. "At least there are people there and we can talk." Then she added, "Nobody ever says anything worth hearing and I usually wish I had stayed home, but what am I to do?" Her name is legion, and millions of lonely men and women, dissatisfied with themselves, seek to escape in bars and taverns everywhere.

We want and need recognition and response from others and some sense of belonging, but comfortable relationships are thwarted by our own interior discomfort. We hunger for caring fellowship that is more than superficial, and yet our own lack of inscape security thwarts our quest. We may seek escape from our aloneness in the cocktail set, most of whom are as lonely and inwardly restless as we. We soon discover, however, that we are by no means satisfied by comradeship stimulated by Scotch and soda.

If in recognition of ourselves as social beings we try to adjust ourselves to the standards of those who frequent bars and cocktail lounges, we drive ourselves into deeper isolation because we do violence to our inscapes. Our identity as persons is threatened because we allow ourselves to be "other-directed" for the sake of fellowship. A college student made the point when he said, "I get along in my fraternity by going along, but I can't put myself into it." There was something in him rebelling against "going along," something of his own integrity which left him feeling he did not really belong.

Sinclair Lewis' Babbitt voiced the hazard of going along, adjusting to the requirements of a superficial society when he confessed sadly, "I've never done a single thing I've wanted to do in my whole life."[11] He adjusted himself to the mores and patterns of Main Street, to its shoddy values and its casual ethic until there was nothing left that was himself. He was like a billiard ball, responding to whatever pressures pushed him this way or that. The fellowships he knew were the essence of superficiality, and inwardly he was desperately lonely.

In drifting with the social tide we sacrifice the integrity of the inscape which is so essential to all rewarding fellowship. We come to the condition of J. Alfred Prufrock, pictured graphically by T. S. Eliot. Prufrock, coasting along with the tide, was a sad and introverted little man. He suggests the modern, feeling deeply, yet rendered impotent by the loss of old faiths and firm convictions that once provided a reason for existence and a solid core for the inscape. Prufrock knows only a heap of broken images. His sanctuary, like his heart, is empty. He says in protest,

> I should have been a pair of ragged claws
> Scuttling across the floors of silent seas.[12]

He longs for something more than superficial fellowship and for life that is more than "other-directed."

We are, to be sure, social beings, but our capacity for creative personal relationships depends on the integrity and security of the inscape. It is the God-directed whose lives are anchored solidly in values that endure beyond time and tide who are able to relate vitally to others.

DIRECTION AND PURPOSE

The stability of the inscape in all of us demands a sense of direction, worthy goals, and high purpose. We are, like all nature, made for growth, "first the blade, then the ear, then the full grain in the ear."[13] Jan Smuts was right in his insistence that the universe is busy creating wholes and nature is dissatisfied with the unfinished. There is a gentle conspiracy of nature turning the rosebud into the full-blown rose. Or, to put it another way, as does Henry N. Wieman, God is "the growing good" in friendship, love, or beauty. He is the emerging good in character that is integrated, other-concerned, and courageous.

Whenever we retreat into inertia and cease to grow we inhibit the inner flow of things and defy what is deepest in nature. We divorce ourselves from the source of meaning for our lives when we drift without a sense of direction. Essentially, we are instruments of God born to fulfill our possibilities in the service of the noblest and the best we know. It is, of course, as purposeful beings that we are "connected up" to the source of all significance and value in a universe that is forever engaged in creating wholes. It is as drifters, going nowhere, that we blunder into lonely isolation from all that makes life worth living.

In his *The Life of Solitude,* Petrarch insists that "To have a single aim, sure and steadfast is the mark of the wise man; inconstancy of purpose is the most certain proof of folly."[14] He goes on to say that the "single aim" to be valid necessarily is related to the spiritual and moral aspirations of man as an instrument of God. He cautions against random running here and there under the illusion that we are serving God by being merely busy. We need to beware lest we are "shattered against the rocks of human activities."

Without spiritual and moral purpose we drift and blunder and our sense of direction is fouled. With clear intentions we find our lives meaningful and our human relations significant. At sixty-eight a vital and radiant woman wrote:

I have an idea at the moment. I want to learn Braille next year so I can work with the blind. I have seen such pathetic cases recently of people in their eighties who can't see to read any more and life seems so empty for them. If I could read Braille and help them to learn to read, it would be such a comfort to them. Who knows, I too may be eighty some day.[15]

Needless to say, the continuing purposefulness of the woman's life has made her life meaningful and enriched her fellowship with those she is seeking to help. By way of her ever-expanding goals she is vitally related to the Source of her spiritual vitality.

It is in purposeful living that we escape from the fetters of loneliness even in the midst of hardship and suffering. Karl Augustus Menninger, for example, describes his experience meeting doctors who had been imprisoned at Buchenwald.[16] Menninger was with the American troops who liberated the prisoners of Hitler's hate. Throughout their imprisonment, the doctors were surrounded by suffering and death. Around them men died by the thousands. The doctors, like other prisoners, were up at 4 A.M., answering roll calls, toiling on the Autobahn, answering roll calls again, and finally finishing the days with bowls of thin soup.

The doctors were starved, beaten, and overworked like the others, with no reason to expect any other fate than the miserable death and cremation which they observed about them daily.

Yet there was a difference between the doctors and the others. At night, when the other prisoners were asleep, these thin, hungry, weary doctors got up, huddled together and talked. They discussed cases. They organized a medical society. They prepared and presented papers. They made plans for improving health conditions. Then they began to smuggle in materials to make medical instruments. And finally, they built, of all things, an X-ray machine. They spent every moment of their time ministering to the prisoners, using their talents under incredible difficulties to care for other people.

What sustained these gallant men? They fulfilled their destiny as purposeful beings. They were instruments of God serving their fellow prisoners. There were no crowds to cheer their triumph, no newspapers to proclaim their greatness, there was nothing but their inner commitment to each other, to their fellow prisoners, and to God. And they came through, emaciated, half dead, but gloriously triumphant. They knew, even in the midst of degradation, that their lives had meaning and value.

FAITH

Our capacity to cope with aloneness and to find meaning for our lives despite difficult circumstances and a lonely landscape depends on the aliveness of our minds, the integrity and purposefulness of our hearts, and the faith that inhabits the inscapes we call our own. Faith is more than a correct creed, more than knowledge of the Scriptures or faithfulness in prayer, important as these are. Faith is "the assurance of things hoped for, the conviction of things not seen."[17] It is an awareness that the shadows of personal existence come and go against a background that holds together and is endlessly dependable. It is the conviction that God is involved with us in all of our struggles to effect the growth of love and truth, beauty and goodness, justice and righteousness.

Faith does not stand alone in isolation from our common life and it is by no means divorced from "the daily round, the common task." By faith we hold fast to the moral values that undergird our life together. We risk the venture of love on the assumption that love, even for the unlovable, is better than hate. We hazard our lives on truth in the firm faith that integrity is more worthy than deceit. We risk compassion in the certainty that tenderness is wiser than cruelty. By faith we know we ought to be honest, true, pure, good, not because honesty, truth, and goodness are good policy, but because they are realistic requirements in the Kingdom of God.

We risk deception and violence, hatred, and even cruelty only if our ethical values are merely conventions. Confidence is shattered and fellowship is broken if we have no consensus concerning right and wrong "under God." On the other hand, we are able to trust each other if we both trust God. We are able to do business with each other with confidence when we both believe in God as the ground of our being. We are aware that it is difficult for us to deal with Communists whose values hinge not on God, but on the state. Right is whatever is useful to the cause of revolution. Wrong is anything that thwarts the progress of the Marxian dream. There are no absolutes; long live the relative.

Our hope of trusting fellowships rests, therefore, on commonly accepted ideals flowing from our faith in God. Some things we are constrained to know by faith. Carl Sandburg used to tell how in his younger days he enjoyed riding on a train, in the smoking car, in a seat back of the "deadheads," the railroaders going back to home base. They talked freely and easily as a rule. Once, however, a young fireman in overalls took a seat and slouched down comfortably. After a time a brakeman in a blue uniform came along and planted himself alongside the fireman. They said nothing and did not even look at each other.

Minutes passed, then the brakeman, looking straight ahead, said, "Well, what do you know today?" and he kept on looking ahead until he turned abruptly and stared at the fireman, adding, "for sure?" It was a pertinent question: "What do you know today—for sure?" The answer came. It was slow and honest, "Not a damn thing."

There are, however, some things the inscape must know "for sure." We need to know that no matter what transpires around us, there are some things that "cannot be shaken and remain." If violence erupts and conflict comes, there still are ethical "keepsakes, lasting beyond hunger and death." It is in our knowing "for sure" that we find the basis for the life of fellowship. We must believe on pain of drifting into chaos.

Life always is and always will be a venture into the unknown for us as believing beings. We move into our tomorrows by faith or we do not move at all. Faith is the courage to risk the uncertainty with confident hope. It says "Yes" to the venture despite the anxiety of "No." It doesn't remove the "No" of doubt. As Paul Tillich says, "It does not build a castle of doubt-free security," but it does remove the fear to venture.

There is a suggestive note in the story of the disciples rowing their boat on the Sea of Galilee with high winds against them. They were making no progress in the dark and they expected to be swamped by the storm. The story reports that Jesus came to them walking on the water and they were afraid and cried out for fear, thinking He was a ghost. He reassured them and, so the account continued, "immediately the ship was at the land to which they were going."[18] They got nowhere against the storm until Jesus stepped in. Then they were where they wanted to go.

More often than not we are like the disciples, caught in storms of hostility and conflict, struggling in futility and anxiety until God steps in. It is not that the landscape is altered so that we are able to have our own way. It is rather that the inscape surrenders to the demands for love and integrity. We remember the things we can know "for sure," and in quiet trust we find the way toward the life of community wherein we all need each other.

We All Need Each Other

Now and then we are reminded pointedly how much we all need each other. When ice storms or floods, tornadoes or strikes upset the normal tenor of our lives we discover we are by no means self-sufficient. When electric power lines are down we are unable to remedy matters ourselves. When telephone service is cut off we discover that communications hinge on other people. If we are isolated by deep snow we may have to be rescued by helicopter. Again and again we have illustrations of the contemporary truth of the ancient word of Ecclesiastes, "Two are better than one because . . . if they fall one will lift up his fellow; but woe to him who is alone when he falls and has not another to lift him up."[1]

INTERDEPENDENCE

We are not now nor were the ancients altogether self-sufficient. Our lives are mutually intertwined and the more complicated our civilization becomes the more we are dependent on other people for life and livelihood. The strike of a few thousand railroad workers could so paralyze the transportation system that in a short time we would be hungry. Building would stop for lack of steel. Homes would be darkened for lack of coal to turn the generators producing electricity for power and light. Before too long the economy that sustains our lives would come to a grinding halt. We are, whether we wish it or not, dependent on those who are involved in sustaining life.

Now and then we are disposed to wish for what we call "the good old days" when our fathers were not, or did not seem to be, so dependent on other people. The pioneers lived on their own plots of ground, made their own clothes, raised their own food, and managed to sustain life by their own toil and intelligence. Of course, whether they knew it or not, they, too, were dependent on others. They used plows others fashioned and seed-corn grown by someone else. There were those who made saddles for their horses, guns for their hunting, and provided the cooking utensils they used to prepare their food.

If we push back through the centuries looking for men who were self-sufficient we are inclined to say, "Just look at Columbus," alone on the sea in his little ship. But Columbus was involved in a vast partnership of ideas, techniques, and experience. He did not discover the compass that guided him over trackless seas. He was a debtor to sailors before him who had learned the art of sailing and the craft of building solid ships. Columbus was a debtor to many men before he landed on the shores of a new continent.

The work we do from day to day always is work somebody else has done. We begin where they left off. And, of course, someone else will begin where we stop. We inherit "great and goodly cities" we did not build, "and houses full of all good things" we never gathered, "and cisterns hewn out" that we never dug, and "vineyards and olive trees" that we did not plant.[2] So spoke the Deuteronomist when he sought to make his people aware of their indebtedness to the past and to the toilers of the present who made their way of life possible.

We all need each other, the toilers in the quarries and the men who sand and salt the icy highways; the farmers who sow and harrow and the men who drive the buses on our busy streets; the teachers who teach our children and the men who find the oil that drives planes and ships and motorcars; the lawyers who gird our "liberty in law" and the newsmen who keep us informed. We do not live or stand alone, but rather among a vast crowd of toilers who lift us by their labor.

More ties than we can number bind us to our fellows near and far. We are as close to foreign neighbors as the nearest airstrip. Trouble in Berlin or Saigon, the Congo or the Middle East has repercussions in Washington, Chicago, and in the little towns that dot the nation. The school dropout in Chicago may well be the thief in the suburb, so that we in the suburbs are involved in what happens in the schools of the Windy City. All of us are involved in mankind, not as islands, but as part of the main. What happens in Montgomery or Selma, Alabama, has repercussions throughout the world, stirring anger in Cairo, Leopoldville, and Delhi.

We are living in a world in which we cannot afford animosities or hostilities. Our need for each other imposes on us the necessity for working and living in harmony with each other.

GIFTS

When we look into our own lives it is clear, too, that however much pride rebels, we are not self-made. We are the consequence of our comradeships and human contacts, our friendships and affections. We do not, indeed, cannot stand alone against the world. Even Ulysses, who was anything but humble, sensed how intimately his life was intertwined with those about him. Speaking for the legendary King of Ithaca, Tennyson wrote,

> I am become a name
> For always roaming with an hungry heart.
> Much I have seen and known, . . .
> I am a part of all I have met.[3]

Such is the truth, of course, "I am a part of all I have met," but in a deeper sense all I have met is part of me. The living and the dead have conspired to make us what we are. It may be true, as philosophers contend, that John Locke was only partly right when he said that the mind is like a blank sheet of paper upon which the impressions of sense are written, but surely our lives bear the marks of many who came our way,

> Ships that pass in the night, and speak each other in passing.[4]

Faith, hope, and courage are mostly not our own but are the gifts of those with whom we traveled through some "valley of the shadow." The wisdom of others lingers in the insights we have won. Their faith endures within our hearts like anchors to windward when storms blow in from the deep. Their courage lies beneath our surface and seeming and is the often undiscovered hero of the soul.

When the course of our human relationships runs smoothly, lubricated by affection and trust in each other and in God, there is a rich bequest of value that we give to one another. However, when our human contacts are twisted by conflict and the absence of trust, each party to the conflict robs the other of some portion of himself. The wise man becomes the fool; the calm becomes the cantankerous. The very unity of ourselves is shattered by the strife in which we are involved. The delicate mechanisms of the body are set askew by tension and we are beset by nervous indigestion and insomnia. Our powers to reason wisely are nullified by indignation and we are tempted to see no good in those who thwart our will.

So it is that the status of our human relationships bears heavily upon us. If our affections enrich our lives, our animosities make us poor; if our loves are a benediction, our hates are a curse. If our trust in one another is a blessing, our fear and mistrust leave us haunted by lonely insecurity. How we relate to one another determines how we are able to cope with life, whether we are beset by acid indigestion or stabilized by peace of mind and heart.

"I have been physically ill, unable to keep anything on my stomach ever since my husband and I became estranged," said a distraught woman. Heaven only knows how many ulcers have been born in conflicts at home or at the office, or how many heart attacks have come from animosities and frictions. We are by no means immune to the day-by-day irritations that brood in our labors side by side. We become a part of all we have met, and if we have met conflict and animosity along the way we bear their scars in body and in mind.

DEBILITATING HOSTILITY

Jesus was acutely aware of the hazardous hostilities that divide us one from another. They provoke problems in homes and churches, in business enterprises and in social organizations. He knew, too, that personal animosities separate us from God and leave us isolated and anxious in what appears to us to be not the best but the worst of all possible worlds.

In the Sermon on the Mount Jesus had a great deal to say about the necessity for creative human relationships. Worship, He knew, is enfeebled by personal hostilities, and the significance of giving is nullified by unresolved conflicts. "Therefore if you are offering your gift at the altar," Jesus said, "and there remember that your brother has something against you, leave your gift at the altar and go; first be reconciled to your brother, and then come and offer your gift."[5] Personal animosities, so it seems, are an affront to God.

Using typical Oriental imagery and exaggeration in order to make His point clear, Jesus expanded the commandment, "You shall not kill"[6] to include, "One who is angry with his brother shall be liable to judgment."[7] What is more, if you insult your neighbor or call him a fool you shall be "liable to the hell of fire."[8] He is saying to us all, "Watch your human relationships. They are the road to heaven or hell." When we think about the matter soberly we know full well that He was right.

A friend of mine used to say sourly, "Hell is other people." He might better have said that hell is wrong relations with other people. Nothing so completely reduces us to protoplasm seething with inner turmoil as animosity toward another person. The man who starts for his office in the morning after a tiff with his wife is in a state of anguished tension that makes a shambles of his day. An office quarrel sends a man home in such a state of inner disarray that he is poor company for his wife and children. "Hell is," indeed, "wrong relations with other people."

Sometimes we say, "I'm so mad, I can't see straight." The observation is profoundly true. When we are filled with hostility and anger we do not "see straight." Studies suggest that the angry motorist is accident prone, and so is the angry pedestrian. One of the problems in army gunnery is inner hostility. Our army tanks, for example, are equipped with complicated range-finding mechanisms. The gunner sights his target, finds out how far away it is, and tracks it for accurate fire.

The man who uses the range finder needs what is known as depth vision so that he can judge distance. Unfortunately, his personal life bears on his vision. Arguments, scoldings, feelings of hostility have an effect on how he sees. A morning tongue lashing at the breakfast table can throw the gunner's depth vision a hundred yards off target. Perhaps more serious is the fact that a driver passing cars on the highway after an argument with his boss can misjudge distance so much as to invite a head-on collision.

Anger and hostility involve widespread physiological effects. One part of the nervous system is active only when we are experiencing fear or anger. When we feel hostility it begins to function. As a throwback to our primitive past, it prepares us for physical struggle. It halts digestion and rushes blood to the muscles, arms, and legs. The heartbeat increases its rate, and we are prepared to fight. The modern world, however, frowns on fighting, so we do not fight. Maybe we grip the steering wheel tighter, grind our teeth, and seethe inside. In any event, the processes of the body are disrupted and the nervous system takes a beating. As a consequence, we are not ourselves.

Obviously, under the stress of hostility our spiritual temperature is decisively lowered. Love and good will make their exit and God seems entirely remote. God is wherever love brings a benediction, wherever forgiveness heals a wound, wherever tenderness yields a blessing. On the other hand, God is banished from the scene wherever hostility broods with bitterness and anger seethes within.

CAUSES OF HOSTILITY

Psychologically, the hostilities that divide us from one another have four basic causes. The first is thwarted wishes, being prevented from doing what we want to do. There are those whose tolerance for the frustration of their wishes is very small. Their boiling point is low and when what they want is denied, they react with instant antagonism to whoever and whatever stands in their way.

There was, for example, the man whose automobile would not

start the night he wanted to go to the theater. In a rage he drove his fist through the windshield. The shattered glass severed an artery and he bled to death before he could be taken to a hospital. His behavior, of course, was irrational and foolish, but it is an illustration of an angry reaction to thwarted wishes. The object of his hostility was inanimate, but he dealt with it as if a balky motor were capable of personal feelings.

We sometimes bump into a chair or table, bruising a shin, and then go back and kick whatever got in the way, thereby intensifying our own pain. In business our wishes for a promotion or an increase in salary are thwarted and, because we cannot kick the object of our irritation, we express hostility to whoever is nearest at hand. It may be a wife, a customer, or a friend. But our anger is basically the result of thwarted wishes.

Again, hostility often is engendered by wounded vanity. It was Bismarck who wrote in 1871, "We are a vain folk, irritated even by not being able to display our vanity." There are those who react to criticism with anger. Their vanity is wounded because someone punctures their proud assumptions of competence. Even those who "speak the truth in love," as Paul wrote, are greeted with hostility.

Then, too, vanity is injured by the necessity of playing second fiddle while somebody else is taking all the accolades. Often the elder child in a family reacts with hostility and sullenness when a baby brother or sister arrives. He has been the center of attention, the apple of his mother's eye, and suddenly he is thrust into the background while everyone gives attention to the new arrival. Psychologists say that a considerable number of first-born children cannot forgive their parents for what they regard as "rejection" by the appearance of a brother or sister. The injury to their self-esteem and vanity makes them sullen and resentful. The new arrival is the serpent in their infant paradise.

There is a reasonable facsimile of what happens to a first-born youngster in many businessmen whose vanity is wounded when the company brings in an outsider to fill some coveted position. The intruder becomes an object of hostility that is deep-seated and can be of murderous intensity. The wounded vanity of those who are condemned to second-fiddle status when they are sure they ought to be first fiddle is a source of major conflicts.

The third major cause of hostility is what we regard as injustice to ourselves or our friends. An angry woman once denounced her aunt in scathing terms because, as she said, "I cared for her for ten years and then she left all her money to my brother." She was outraged by the feeling she had been unjustly treated. The fact that she seemed to have a right to be angry over the turn of events did not help.

Violence, riots, and demonstrations on our city streets are the product of hostility born of resentment against injustices imposed upon the Negro by the white community. The unreasoned shouts of Negroes gone berserk in Los Angeles, "Burn," "Kill," were the product of explosive hostility and hatred. Dr. Martin Luther King's doctrine of nonviolent protest could not contain the fury of angry men and women, whose fury hurt themselves more than it hurt anyone else.

The fact that the riot in Los Angeles was spontaneous and without leadership suggests the latent feelings of hostility in millions of Negroes in the ghettos of the United States. Theirs was a revolt of rising expectations that had been thwarted. The hopes inspired by civil rights laws proved to have been extravagant. Laws could not create jobs for the unskilled or better housing for those without financial resources.

Hopeless, frustrated, lonely in their lostness, Negroes in their overcrowded slums provide all the ingredients for spontaneous violence. The feeling that the white community does not care begets resentment. Lack of communication between white and Negro leads to misunderstanding and bitterness. Even though Negro and white need each other in our complex society, the two are divided by hostility wrought by a century of discrimination and injustice.

Recent studies suggest, too, a rising mood of hostility in teenagers and a revolt against authority. Even in affluent communities there are teen-age youngsters feeling the injustice of having to grow up in loveless homes. They express their hostility by smashing car windows, slashing tires, and defying accepted sex mores. They hate both themselves and the world and try to find a way out by indulging in liquor and drugs.

Magazines and newspapers have reported the escapades of hostile youngsters crashing parties to which they were not invited, smashing furniture and windows, and cracking heads with baseball bats. Loveless and lonely, they fight back against the feeling that they are outsiders with violence, disorder, drag races, and varied escapades which show their defiance of authority.

Hostility born of real or imagined injustice breaks out in a thousand forms in our contemporary society. Newspapers now and then receive letters saying: "Cancel my subscription to your paper. Your reporting of my candidate's campaign has been unfair and unjust." And during political campaigns, particularly those that arouse emotions, hostilities are generated that sometimes hang on for months or years. We become angry over real or imagined unfairness.

There is, then, a fourth source of hostility, namely self-hate that turns outward. The biography of Sinclair Lewis describes the author of *Main Street, Babbitt,* and *Elmer Gantry,* as a man with a chip on his shoulder. Because he hated himself, he poured the venom of his self-hate on those around him. The same thing can be said of Karl Marx. It was Carl Schurz who said of Marx, "I never have seen a man whose bearing was so provoking and intolerable." His self-hate spilled over both on those who collaborated with him and those who opposed him.

It is a simple and incontrovertible fact that if we hate ourselves we cannot love others. If we lack respect for ourselves we are bound to be at enmity with others. The proper kind of self-respect is necessary if we are to love others and treat them with good will and consideration.

RECONCILIATION

Our hostilities, untamed, are decidedly dangerous, and we are constrained to deal with them. As Mark Twain wrote, "What a man sees in the human race is merely himself in the deep and honest privacy of his own heart." If we feel hostile, bitter, and angry, we see other people as hostile, bitter, and angry. Our human relationships are a reflection of our own inner feelings and attitudes.

The prayer of Violet Alleyn Story is appropriate for all of us,

> Keep me from bitterness. It is so easy
> To nurse sharp, bitter thoughts each dull dark hour.
> . . . .
> Help me to harvest a new sympathy
> For suffering humankind, a wiser pity
> For those who lift a heavier cross with Thee.[9]

So, if we are at odds with our environment, hostile and bitter, we had best begin by looking into ourselves and dealing with our hostilities and our inner bitterness.

Possibly what we want, we should not have, or maybe we need to accept the necessity for playing a high-grade second fiddle. Perhaps the injustice we feel is more imagined than real. If it is real, we gain nothing by violent protest. We only hurt ourselves. If it is imagined, we had best take a sober look at ourselves. It is possible that our own self-hate has obscured our vision of other people. At any rate, when our hostilities have made a shambles of our lives there is no place to begin except with ourselves.

Maybe it is pride or vanity, I'm not sure, that keeps us from going to those who feel hostile to us or to whom we feel hostile. But Jesus, without asking who is wrong or who is right, says, if "your brother has something against you, . . . go . . . be reconciled to your brother."[10] It is not easy, but nothing creative in the way of human relations ever comes about until somebody takes the road of reconciliation. The words, "I'm sorry," come hard, but often they yield a benediction.

We have a choice, a choice between rebellion and reconciliation. Harry Overstreet notes wisely that the Nazi movement under Hitler was an example of hostility-born rebellion against society. All the defeated, the frustrated, the angry young men and women rallied around the crooked cross and expressed their anger and hostility in violence. They magnified their insignificant selves goose-stepping with the party.

A similar process is in evidence today among Communist

groups. Here again the motive for identifying with the group is hostility, generating rebellion. Belonging to the party and following the party line the individual member can revel in "holy hate." The party, chiefly engaged in invective, provides an outlet for the animosity and bitterness of the individual. And wherever there are hate groups, in revolt against the church, the government, the established institutions of society, there are men and women expressing their hostility with invective.

Bottled hate sometimes explodes into murder that from the outside seems incredible. It expresses itself in unexplained acts of violence. It shatters the harmony of social groups and at times leaves us gasping and incredulous. It divides our homes and we are at a loss to understand what has happened.

The alternative is reconciliation, willingness to "go" and "be reconciled" to those from whom we are divided by hostility. It is a possibility only when someone who feels wronged is willing to risk going with forgiveness in his heart, or when someone, aware of his division from another, accepts the challenge to seek understanding and renewal of fellowship.

Recently in Berlin, Germany, I met with a group of young people from Coventry, England. Coventry, you may recall, was battered and broken by Nazi bombs during World War II, and the beautiful Coventry Cathedral was destroyed. But the young people I met were on their way to Dresden in East Germany, a city smashed into rubble by Allied bombs toward the end of the war. They were on their way to help clear the ruins and rebuild a hospital the bombs had destroyed. What is more, they had brought money, part of it contributed by the British airmen who had participated in the destruction of Dresden, to help rebuild the hospital. Significantly, the visit of the young people to Dresden came in response to a delegation of young people from West Germany who had gone to Coventry to build a youth center there to make amends for the destruction their fathers had wrought.

There is hope in reconciliation, a healing of the wounds of hostility and bitterness. It is a confession of our need for each other, a way to move beyond loneliness to fellowship and understanding. "We felt we had to do something to help bring understanding and fellowship between the East and the West," said one young man from Coventry. "Maybe it won't do any good, but at least it is worth a try."

Our world today is in desperate need of men and women who will risk trying the way of reconciliation. It is crying in its agony for those who will do justly, love mercy, and walk humbly with God. There are no barriers to brotherhood that cannot be penetrated by men and women of good will who know that in the economy of God we all need each other. There are no hostilities that cannot be overcome by those who believe it is worth trying to bring understanding and fellowship into our tortured society.

All of us are wounded at one time or another by someone else, and all of us hurt others now and then. How can we avoid bitterness? By acceptance of the fact that all of us are infected by the virus of sin and self-centeredness. How can we avoid repression that bottles our hostility inside? By love that makes allowances for the sins of others and at the same time is honest about the self. How can we avoid hating? By forgiveness generated by the knowledge that we too are in need of forgiveness. As Jesus summarized the truth, "Forgive us our debts [sins], as we also have forgiven our debtors" [those who have sinned against us].[11]

After struggling with resentful bitterness against a business colleague who won a coveted promotion, a man and his wife came to the conclusion that their resentful hostility was ruining their relationship to each other. They decided something had to be done. He went to his colleague to say, "I've been resentful ever since you were promoted. I'm sorry, and from now on I'll do everything I can to help you succeed." It was not easy, but it meant reconciliation and renewed fellowship.

SHARING

When we are reconciled to one another, our hostilities banished, we are able to share our ventures, our hopes, and our fears, and we are made richer and wiser, better and more stable by our sharing. One thing every woman knows is that shopping is an ordeal made bearable if at the day's end she is able to show her purchases to an appreciative audience. The hat she bought with some trepidation becomes a thing of beauty if her husband says, "It looks quite perfect on you." The quiet sharing and approval banish tiredness and bring renewal.

The small boy sounded a solid note when he said to his mother that he wished she would take a planned trip during Christmas vacation instead of in March "because who would I show my homework to?" When learning is shared it is blessed. When homework is approved it brings contentment and a feeling of accomplishment. Youngsters are lonely and insecure when there is no one to share the toil of learning, to approve their triumphs, and to encourage them when they fail.

In a hundred ways sharing multiplies our joy in living. A college student, sent home by the college physician to be checked for an operation that might be necessary, went to the home hospital for a check-up. Examinations indicated there was no need for an operation, whereupon the young man said to his mother: "I'm sure glad you are here, Mother. It's nice to have somebody to be happy with." Sharing multiplied the joy he felt.

Franz Schubert noted his need for the shared life at a time when his fortunes were at a low ebb. "Dear Schober," he wrote to a cherished friend, "I hear you are not happy. You have to sleep off the plague of despair—so Schwind tells me. Although I regret so much hearing this, I am, however, not surprised, as it is the fate of every rational being in this miserable world. And what should we do with happiness since misfortune is the only spur we have left to us? If only you, Schwind, Kuppel, and I were together, then misfortunes would not bother us. As it is, we are separated, each of us in a separate corner."[12]

Being in separate corners where we cannot share our mutual woes and joys leaves us vulnerable to despair and robs us of life's challenge. Even animals react unhappily to isolation. So a five-year experiment at McGill University laboratory made clear.[13] One group of seven Scottish terrier puppies was reared normally. Another group of terrier puppies, eleven in all, was isolated, one dog to each cage. The restricted puppies had no communication with each other. Food and drink were given through sliding panels, so that they did not see human beings. The experimental puppies were kept in isolation until they were seven to ten months old.

When the hitherto isolated puppies were exposed to the same exercises and stimulation as the normal puppies, they were confused and bewildered. The psychologists conducting the experiment discovered that when the dogs were exposed to a toy car which, when touched, caused an electric shock, the normal dogs learned very quickly to avoid the car. "In contrast," wrote the experimenters, "the restricted dogs behaved wildly and aimlessly. They jumped about and galloped in circles." After two years the once isolated dogs still had difficulty in learning.

Even dogs need normal dog relationships in which their experience is shared. Isolation is a deterrent to the learning process and to normal adjustment to the circumstances of life.

If we are inclined to wonder why Communism wins so many converts in spite of its tyrannies and persecutions, there is a clue in the words of Simonov, a Russian writer, quoted by President Eisenhower in *Crusade in Europe*. Simonov wrote: "I, personally, cannot bear loneliness. . . . If you ask me what the Soviet System has done for the writer I should answer that, first of all, it has erased from his inner self all sense of loneliness, and given him the feeling of complete and absolute 'belonging' to society and the people."[14]

Living too much in isolation in our competitive society, we miss the sense of belonging to the beloved community. Sharing too little, we become victims of loneliness, and prey to all the neurotic behavior of the isolated puppies. There is healing for us in sharing.

LOVE

We were meant to live in community and in communion with one another, not in isolation. We live as we love; we die as we live in loveless separation from our fellow men. Aldous Huxley, with his usual capacity for paradox, wrote with cynicism tinged with faith: "Of all the worn, smudged, dog's-eared words in our vocabulary, 'love' is surely the grubbiest, smelliest, slimiest . . . it has become an outrage to good taste and decent feeling. . . . And yet it has to be pronounced, for, after all, love is the last word."[15]

Love is the last word because "God is love," and without love we are without God. If we do not love anyone, anywhere, we are desperately alone. The initiative lies with each one of us. As someone remarked, "Those who live to themselves are left to themselves." If we do not love others and open the doors to friendship, those who are around us back away from us.

One of the saddest biographies in American literature is that of Sinclair Lewis by Mark Schorer, who wrote with both sensitivity and appreciation of a distinguished literary figure who was isolated in himself. He noted that Lewis always seemed to walk alone. Now and then when he went out into his garden he always walked in the deep shadows of the north side of the house where he would not be seen. He would walk back and forth in the gloom. Schorer was reminded of a passage in *Our Mr. Wrenn,* in which Lewis had written,

his loneliness shadowed him. Of that loneliness one could make many books; how it sat down with him; how he crouched in his chair, bespelled by it, till he violently rose and fled, with loneliness for a companion in his flight. He was lonely. He sighed he was "lonely as fits." Lonely—the word obsessed him. Doubtless he was a bit mad, as are all isolated men who sit in distant lands longing for the voice of friendship.[16]

Sinclair Lewis was not isolated in a distant land. He was rather isolated in himself. He could neither give nor receive friendship. He could love neither himself nor others. He tried to escape in work, writing until exhaustion overwhelmed him. Then he would lose himself in drink. He lived to himself and consequently was left to himself. There were those who loved him, but he rejected them and retreated into his own self-contained world.

The comment of a young woman under treatment by the psychiatrist, Theodor Reik, goes to the heart of our need. "I can stand physical loneliness quite well," she said, "but emotional loneliness not at all. When I know that there is no one who cares for me, when I don't love anyone, I become gloomily depressed and even desperate."[17] So, indeed, do we all. We all need each other. There is in the human heart an inexhaustible need to love and be loved.

When we are standing shoulder to shoulder, loving one another, we find an added power for life, a plus beyond the mere addition of our several strengths. It comes to us by the courtesy of God. "It is written, 'Man shall not live by bread alone,' "[18] and the words are written not only in the Scriptures, but in the nature of man. We hunger for some intimations of God, some hints of eternity in time. Our hearts cry out for deep affections that bind us to one another and have within them something of the love of God that runs through all and unites all.

The hauntingly humorous observation of a troubled young man suggests the feeling of multitudes. "I walked on Broadway last evening," he said, "and felt depressed and lonely. No girl, no friend, no relative. On the corner of Seventy-Second Street I read an announcement in big letters on the walls of a house. It said, YOU HAVE A FRIEND AT THE CHASE NATIONAL BANK. Well, I thought, I have at least one friend."[19] To have at least one friend somewhere is to find hope and reassurance and some hint of God.

With all the lonely people in the world, all needing each other, how can we be without friends? We need only open the doors and the windows of our lives, offering friendship and affection, and we shall have both in return. We need only to seek those who are lonely and give ourselves to them in self-forgetful kindness and we shall venture beyond loneliness ourselves.

John's account of the Last Supper is revealing because it goes beyond the other gospels in suggesting what concerned Jesus most when He faced the fact of His imminent death. His own expected pain and suffering remained unobtrusively in the background as He talked with His disciples. At the moment when His world was falling apart with hate and bitterness, He was thinking of the one thing that could hold the world together. There in the Upper Room, as He broke bread with the disciples He said to them, "This is my commandment, that you love one another as I have loved you."[20]

We cannot escape our need for each other. We are one with all mankind. As Carl Sandburg said of Abraham Lincoln, "If he was a solitary man, Lincoln could not be presented as desolate. His melancholy grew from a profound, indefinable identification with man's fate, a pensiveness tempered by quiet bravery, and loving insight."[21] There may be for all of us hours of lonely melancholy to be assuaged by an awareness that we are identified with man's fate and to be made endurable by bravery and loving insight.

4

Strange Estrangement

I
N THE BEGINNING," so the story runs, God created a man and called him Adam. He must have been a lonely soul, wandering in the Garden of Eden with nobody anywhere to understand his feelings or to share his fate. The Lord God was mindful of Adam's plight, and He said, "It is not good that man should be alone; I will make him a helper fit for him." So, the Lord "passed a miracle," as the angel said in *The Green Pastures,* and formed a woman from the rib of Adam, and Adam and Eve began their life together.

Like the Lord in the story of creation, we know it is not good to be alone. Needing each other, we link our lives in marriage. As the Psalmist wrote, God "gives the desolate a home to dwell in."[1] And it would be a terribly lonely world without homes and families, without the affection and trust of a venture in togetherness. It would be a frightful world without the comradeship of kindred minds, building homes, and rearing children.

So it is that in our comtemporary world Adam goes a-wooing and Eve sets her cap for Adam. They meet somewhere, at college, on a bus, in an office, or at a party, and Adam is sure he cannot live without his Eve and vice versa. The courting goes on for months or years. There are dreams of home and children and life lived happily ever after the marriage vows are said. The engagement, long or short, is a time of wonder and of joy. Then, in anticipation of Utopia, Adam and Eve settle down to live together.

SEPARATE IDENTITIES: HUSBAND AND WIFE

Usually things go well for a while, settling an apartment or a house, planning and dreaming of the future. The glow of the romance lingers as each explores the other. Problems and differences are brushed under the table. She tries to hide her disappointments and to assure herself that love will overcome. He ignores the little irritations he did not expect. In all probability they avoid discussing the things they wish were different. Each retreats a little into himself, more unconsciously than consciously. Into their relationship comes a strange and gnawing estrangement. It is not a matter of overt conflict, but rather a feeling of isolation.

Adam and Eve have not ceased to love each other, but somehow their expectations have not been entirely fulfilled. Emotionally they feel indispensable to each other, and yet their lines of communication with each other seem to have been slightly impaired. Each had expected to be able to communicate his deepest feelings to the other, but neither is quite able to manage it. Their separate memories and experiences leave them inescapably isolated from each other.

There are times when they seem to be at one with each other, their sense of isolation lost in a river of oneness. They feel the warmth and the goodness of intimate communion, as if they had been made for each other. Then the spell is broken, and each wanders in his separate star. There seems to be a gulf between them that even love and trust cannot cross. They enjoy each other's company. They have no wish to separate. But a strange estrangement is there, as if something in each of them were impenetrable to the other.

In their immaturity they do not know that loneliness is part of their human portion. They do not understand that two people, no matter how much they are in love, never are able completely to merge their separate identities. Each is troubled by the independence of the other, even though they know that independence is healthy. Still each yearns for a closeness, a oneness that never is quite full enough. They cannot seem to preserve the perfect harmony and togetherness they dreamed would be theirs.

Edward, in *The Cocktail Party,* defined the feeling when he said,

> There was a door
> And I could not open it. I could not touch the handle.
> Why could I not walk out of my prison?
> What is Hell? Hell is oneself,
> Hell is alone, the other figures in it
> Merely projections. There is nothing to escape from
> And nothing to escape to. One is always alone.[2]

We are always alone, even when we move from solitariness into families. There is a door we cannot open, try as we will. Our prison is ours, our own separate identity, and we never fully escape from it.

Adam and Eve try various expedients to escape their essential aloneness. Either he or she may develop a confining possessiveness, bordering on neurotic jealousy. Eve may conclude that any interest of Adam outside herself is a threat and a danger. Her motto becomes, "You must love me exclusively." Any interest or affection which must be shared is too much to be endured. Unhappily, such possessiveness increases estrangement rather than oneness.

Or, it may be that one or the other of the partners to the marriage concludes there is something wrong with himself. He may indulge in a splurge of self-centered introspection. He wonders, "What's the matter with me that I can't get through to the one I love?" So, he begins peeling himself like an onion, assuming that when he gets to the last layer he will discover what the onion really is. All that remains, however, is a mystery.

Lenore Marshall, who writes poetry with distinction and authenticity, struggles with the problem of identity in a painful and difficult quest for the self. One verse of hers suggests the essential aloneness she found after peeling the onion. She wrote that she

> Invented a person named I
> With a place of its own
> A certain thing to be done,
> And in fear for that one.[3]

The self in her running fable in quest of identity is elusive and unpredictable, not to be grasped by reason. Her question, and ours, "What's wrong with me?" when a sense of isolation has us in its grip leads to little more than depression.

That is not to say that some self-examination is not appropriate when we find ourselves estranged from those we love. It is to say that excessive self-searching leads not to freedom but to depression. Sooner or later we have no choice but to accept the essential loneliness of our human predicament and to communicate and share as richly as we are able within the limits of our humanness.

CHILDREN AND THE HOME

There are subtle changes that come into our relationship when children invade our privacy. The circle of our affection is expanded to include another lonely ego. It may be that Adam feels at least a little rejected, as if the newborn son or daughter had become the focus of Eve's love and concern. Quiet evenings together are shattered by the wails of a youngster wanting attention. Eve, busy with a multiplicity of tasks, is exhausted by nightfall.

According to *Newsweek,* one Smith College graduate (class of '55), now married, has tacked up in her New York kitchen this phrase from Adlai Stevenson's address at her commencement. Speaking about educated women, he said, "Once they discussed art and philosophy until late at night. Now they are so tired they fall asleep as soon as the dishes are done. Once they wrote poetry, now it's laundry lists." In the early years of marriage there was romance, now there are diapers.

To be sure, children are a joy, or at least they ought to be. Nevertheless, they also involve tiredness and new adjustments between Adam and Eve. If Adam feels a little pushed out and neglected, Eve feels burdened at times and a little resentful that Adam can run out on the home and find escape at the office. Built-in baby sitters are few and far between, and it may be that Eve feels more lonely and confined than before baby blessed her home.

At any rate, there is ample evidence to suggest that young women rearing children in middle- and upper-class families are discontent. A University of Chicago graduate, the mother of three children, summed up her experience by saying, "I'm tired of talking to people three-feet high all day." Conversation with three-foot toddlers is bound to be on an elementary level with little or nothing of deep-level communion in it.

It was Sigmund Freud who noted that "Anatomy is destiny." So women are destined to be mothers and to play the role of kindergarten teachers at home. But, says Dr. Stephen Mamchur, a Wayne State University sociologist and a director of the National Council on Family Relations, there are otherwise intelligent women who are angry "because their husbands cannot become pregnant and do not have to bear children and raise them." They feel trapped and they resent it.

The problem is complicated by two factors, one psychological and the other economic. The first involves the attitude of women toward their role as housewives. There are many who envy the glamour of career women who seem to have the best of all possible worlds. "What do I do?" you hear women ask at class reunions. The response suggests their feeling, "Why, nothing; I'm just a housewife." It is as if they had reduced their place to one of unimportance and insignificance.

The second factor lies in the fact that young executives on the way up are married to their work. As one young housewife remarked, "My husband is simply an overnight guest and a weekend visitor." Like many others of his kind he pushed himself to the limit in his business or profession so that when he came home at night he was too exhausted to do much of anything but read the paper and watch a television western. A young man having trouble at home said sadly, "The competition in business is rugged and when I get home I just don't have what it takes to help wash the dishes and put the children to bed. My wife thinks I'm just shirking my duty."

The truth is that in relation to the first problem, all of us are trapped in one way or another. There is striking testimony to the truth in the novel *The Shoes of the Fisherman* by Morris L. West. It is the story of Kiril Lakota, once a prisoner of the

Communists in Russia and now the pope in Rome. Ruth Lewin asks him, "These stories they print about you, your time in prison, your escape, are they true?" "Yes," he answers, and she goes on, "Now you're in prison again." He nods, "In a way, but I hope to break out of it." Wistfully Ruth continues, "We're all in prison, one way or another."[4] The truth is profound, and those who refuse to accept the fact of their imprisonment suffer most of all.

The housewife with little children is trapped in prison for a while. And yet, the imprisonment can become a benediction. Perhaps, like John Bunyan in Bedford Prison, she can make her prison her "palace beautiful." If contemporary Eves are able to see a little beyond the confinement of the moment to the fruitage of tomorrow they will find meaning in their prisons. If they are able to see tomorrow's character emerging from the problems of today, and the future's wisdom coming from the loneliness of the moment, they find significance in the fact that for a while they are hedged in. The difficulty is that often the small moments of the present are like some minor actor who steals the show and makes the audience miss the lines and action on which the plot hinges. So, the small moments of entrapment steal the show and make Eve miss the lines and action on which the future hinges.

The absence from home of the hard-working father involves the necessity for some compromise in order to avoid estrangement. Quite possibly Adam may be sacrificing too much for too little. His toil is exhausting, to be sure, but the privilege of knowing his children and the value of preserving a creative relationship with Eve are the things that give meaning to his toil. As Jesus asked, "What does it profit a man to gain the whole world and forfeit his life?"[5] Is there any profit in being a world-beater success only to lose the love and affection that make success worth having?

"Women love men and men love their work," is a common saying, but the man who loves his work too exclusively invites loneliness and isolation at home. If he is a victim of status seeking, his economic triumphs may well involve domestic failure; his business success may lead him to the loss of communication on the home front. The problem of young men today is to keep their sense of values straight.

The strange estrangement that so often descends upon homes today multiplies the aloneness of our human predicament. The age of the split-level house also is the age of the split family, and both Adam and Eve are to blame. If they are mature enough to keep their sense of values in perspective and to remember that without love nothing is worth having, they may travel through the years warmly alive and vital, their loneliness made tolerable by their fellowship.

THE ADOLESCENT

If little children are confining, adolescents are a challenge, sometimes more of a challenge than we would wish. If talking with three-foot toddlers leaves us unstimulated, coping with six-foot adolescents with minds of their own is a demanding enterprise. If communicating with little children is relatively easy, communicating with adolescents is a major problem. The adolescent years often are years of strange estrangement from Adam and Eve.

The boy or girl in his teens does not altogether understand himself. He is restless, and both the psychological and physical changes going on inside leave him baffled and lonely. He is quite sure his parents do not understand him. "I wish," said one youngster, "that when adults say the word 'adolescent' they wouldn't assume it is a disease." There are times, certainly, when we who are adults find it difficult to comprehend the ways of teen-agers.

It is curious the way communication between teen-agers and their parents dries up. Often we would give anything we possess to cross the barrier that seems to separate us from our sons and daughters. We know they are troubled, but we cannot get through. We know they are lonely because we are also, and yet they keep their problems and their thoughts to themselves. Only rarely do they let us invade the privacy of their thinking.

The moments of their openness are priceless and rewarding. One high-school youngster arriving home one Saturday night at one o'clock, came into the bedroom of his parents and said: "Mom and Dad, I want to talk to you. I don't want any advice. Just listen." Thereafter, for an hour and a half he talked about school, about his moral concerns, his friends and their parents, and about his religious beliefs. His mother and his father said nothing. They just listened. Then, quite suddenly, the boy got up. "Thanks for listening," he said. "I probably won't talk to you like this again for a year." With that he went to bed.

Whatever agony of isolation there might have been before that episode, there was a moment of wonderful openness and deep communion, of understanding and love. Perhaps here there is a clue to wisdom for those who are parents. It is simply to be receptive and patient, waiting for those moments of openness and communion that, rare though they be, reveal our children and make us aware of their trust and affection. We cannot force them to satisfy either our need or theirs for communication.

Jane Addams once addressed a group of Halsted Street women in Chicago, most of them first generation immigrants, who were having difficulty holding the respect and understanding of their sons and daughters. She told them that when their adolescent youngsters came home from school and wanted to talk with them, they had better stop everything and listen, even if the dinner burned. "Because," she said, "if you don't listen to the little things first, the big things won't come out."

It is in listening to the little things when our youngsters feel in the mood to chat that we create confidence that leads to larger sharing. The wise parental mood is suggested in the sign a young physician hung on his office door, "Small fevers gratefully accepted." Small talk gratefully accepted leads to large matters earnestly shared.

It should be added that when we are baffled by the behavior of our teen-age sons or daughters swooning over the Beatles or playing the role of beatniks, we need to remember the years gone by when our parents were bewildered by our behavior. Recently there was a cartoon in the *Saturday Review* picturing a beatnik and his sweater-girl companion standing nonchalantly on a street corner. Passing by, a portly, middle-aged woman said to her stout, well-dressed husband, "Gordon, look at us twenty-five years ago." That, essentially, is the truth. The youngsters today are ourselves twenty-five or thirty years ago. We may have forgotten our yesterdays and that is unfortunate when we feel estranged from the younger generation today.

Our young people have somewhat more freedom than we had, but we had plenty of liberty to be foolish if we wished. Automobiles were not so common, conversations were a little more restrained, books more subdued, and the motion pictures less blatant. Nevertheless, there were moral cripples then as now. In all probability there are more temptations now than there used to be, but there were plenty when we were young. We were not models of virtue any more than today's children. We need to remember if we expect to have the trust and the confidence of our youngsters.

The senior citizens of our day called us "the lost generation." My grandmother, a staunch Methodist of the old school, could not understand why we were allowed to go to parties without chaperones and plenty of them. She was sure we needed to be watched. She used to say sadly, "It wasn't this way when I was a girl." Not being around when she was a girl, I could not argue the issue. But after reading the history of the period when grandmother was a girl, it seems clear that things really were not as different as she thought. She simply forgot to remember and so intensified her estrangement from me and my generation.

I do not mean to suggest that we are to look with tolerant unconcern upon all the antics of the younger generation. There are times when "No" is the proper answer to an earnest petition, even though the "No" appears to involve intensified estrangement. It is decisively important, however, for Adam and Eve to stand together on the "No." If there are differences of judgment, the matter should be adjudicated in private and a solid front presented to the adolescent. To have a "Yes" from Adam and a "No" from Eve, or vice versa, is fatal, a source of estrangement between parents and an undermined authority for children.

THE CHILD GROWN UP

However difficult the adolescent years, they also are years of rewarding responsibility for parents. We never forget the times of openness and deep communion we have shared with our youngsters, or the joy of seeing them grow toward maturity and responsibility for themselves. It is something of a shock, therefore, when they go off to college, decide to work and have an apartment of their own, or take off to do their stint in the army, navy, or air force.

It is difficult to realize they probably will not be home again to live except for vacations. The adjustment is particularly difficult for mothers who begin to suspect their reason for existence has vanished. All through the years mothers have dedicated themselves to their children's welfare. There were years of driving to and fro from school, cub-scout meetings, boy-scout affairs, Y.M.C.A. functions, and a host of other activities. They seemed exhausting at the time. Even through high school there was the P.T.A. and associated activities, swimming meets, drama club performances, football games, basketball games, and so on. One mother, dividing herself between the activities of three children, remarked, "By the end of the day I feel like a pie—and there just aren't enough slices to go around to everyone."

Then, quite suddenly, it is all over. The pie is not sliced at all. As Jean Ingelow wrote:

> I had a nest full once,
> Oh, happy, happy I;
> Right dearly I loved them,
> But when they were grown,
> They spread out their wings to fly.[6]

The children are gone. Eve's husband is preoccupied with his business, and she is alone. When the children come home from college at Christmas or for the summer, they seem strangely independent. The suggestion, "Hadn't you better wear your overcoat tonight?" is met by the response, "Look, Mom, I've been looking after myself in college all year, and I guess I know whether or not I want my coat." Eve seems strangely unnecessary.

When our children leave home for whatever reason, a subtle change takes place. Thomas Wolfe gave utterance to the paradox in his story, *You Can't Go Home Again.* He wrote of George Webber that "he never had the sense of home so much as when he felt he was going there. It was only when he got there that his homelessness began."[7] Once our children have left it, home never is quite the same again. What is more, their relations with their parents never are quite the same. There is the subtle estrangement of a newly discovered independence. The youngsters are not quite at home at home.

More often than not the youngsters of the collegiate set are ill at ease wherever they are, at home or away from home. They are like the college lad described in *The Cave,* by Robert Penn Warren, who "suddenly felt raw, deprived, and lonely, even if you were a big man on campus, and you stood there and hated your sixty-five dollar rolled-lapel sports jacket from the College Sport Shoppe which looked just like the Ivy League issue of *Esquire* and which today you were wearing to give 'em a treat."[8] Our separateness from our young ones often is due to their own restless ill-at-ease and their inability to break through the barriers of their own sense of aloneness.

We may love our children devotedly and they may respond in kind, but we feel our isolation from them, and when we let our selves think about the way things are, we feel unutterably lonely. If we try to hold our children, they retreat from us. If we seek to hug them close to satisfy our own need, they push us away, gently or otherwise. They cherish their freedom too much to let it go.

If we are wise and willingly set them free to be themselves, we feel the wrench, and yet they love us more for understanding their need to be independent. They respect us for respecting their need. After all, did not we raise them to stand on their own feet, make their own decisions and choices, and fashion their lives with wisdom and dignity? We cannot, in the moment of their independence, snatch it away to assuage our own loneliness.

Nevertheless, it is not easy to let them be free, even when they are married. As one thoughtful Negro woman said, "they are out of my hands now, but they are on my heart." They always are on our hearts and often we ache with loneliness because they are out of the reach of our hands. There is a paradox, however, in the fact that if we let go of them with our hands and rejoice in their independence and freedom, they give us their hearts.

One young man, married less than a year, stopped one morning to visit with his mother over a cup of coffee. In the course of their conversation she asked, "How am I doing as a mother-in-law?" He responded with wisdom beyond his years, "You're doing fine, Mother. Just don't try to be too helpful." We want to be helpful, just as we have tried to be through the years, but too much helpfulness is an invasion of their married independence. They want to be free to find their own way. Trying to be too helpful is an invitation to estrangement.

THE MIDDLE YEARS

So it is that through the later middle years Adam and Eve are back where they started, alone together. In place of their hopes and dreams they have accumulated memories. Instead of children, they have grandchildren. Whereas once they were trying to accumulate things, now they are wondering what they will do with their possessions. In the early years they had energy to burn in dancing and romance, now they are tired by ten o'clock.

The middle years are not easy ones. In business Adam has come to the point of no return. He has not the bright dreams of youth, but rather the knowledge that there is nothing ahead for him except more of the same thing. He has not fulfilled either his dreams or his expectations. The road ahead holds nothing but frustration and plodding on until retirement. Life for him has become prosaic and uninteresting. He is bored with it all.

At the same time, Eve is restless, looking for things to occupy her time. Burdened by a sense of futility compounded by loneliness, she runs from the bridge club to the women's club and on to the drama club or the reading club. One grandmother of fifty confessed sadly, "I'm running madly from one thing to another until I am exhausted trying not to be lonely and useless." She went on, "I've decorated and redecorated my home just to have the feeling that I'm not standing still."

Evenings at home are not exactly festive for Adam and Eve. Maybe they share a TV dinner and then spend the hours until bedtime watching mystery thrillers or Westerns until they feel jaded. Eve may give up and turn in when Adam tunes into a boxing or wrestling match. Nothing they see on the television screen is really stimulating intellectually. They are just killing time, consuming the hours that would be unbearably lonely without Ed Sullivan, "Bonanza," and Perry Mason.

Possibly it is not surprising that the middle years also are the dangerous years. A disturbed woman, involved in an extra-marital affair, explained her adventure by saying, "It never would have happened if I hadn't been so lonely and so bored." The affair, however, was by no means a happy venture. On the contrary, it brought a temporary rapture followed by galling loneliness and remorse. She sailed not into a secure harbor of love and contentment but into stormy waters of disgust and isolation.

Those who are involved in counseling the troubled report there is a growing disposition among the middle-aged to get together in the evenings for cocktails. A thoughtful man observed of one group, "Everybody drinks too much. The men paw the wives of other men and the women seem to like it." He added, "I suppose we all are a little frustrated and lonely and alcohol makes us feel cozy with everybody for a while."

Adam and Eve would not need to feel so cozy and close to other people if they really felt cozy and close to each other. That is the real rub of middle age when of all times there should be a sense of oneness between husband and wife. The road of the years, toiling together, raising children, should provide a sound foundation for oneness and understanding fellowship. It does precisely that if we have kept the lines of communication open, leaning on each other, sharing our successes and failures, our triumphs and disappointments without reservation. But we retreat into ourselves and close the doors of life against each other until we are strangely estranged.

The middle years can be wonderful years for fellowship and growth if, through the years, we have learned to trust each other and to lean on one another. Does it really matter if Adam is not a business tycoon at fifty or fifty-five? One grateful wife remarked, "Jim isn't a howling success, but he is dependable and loyal, and we manage nicely on what he earns." Jim and his wife had put two children through college at considerable sacrifice and Jim had come to the point of no return in his business career, but they had their sense of values straight. They knew what really mattered was not money or possessions but loyalty and dependable love.

Jim's home is not a mansion, but it is a comfortable place with a well-clipped lawn and an attractive garden. Sally seems to enjoy keeping house and she does not mind scrubbing floors and dusting the furniture. She lives for the hour when Jim will be home and they will have the evening together. They enjoy reading, an occasional game of gin rummy, and TV for a while. But they are not bored with each other's company or weary of life. They enjoy seeing their friends to visit or play bridge, but they are not bereft when they are alone together.

Best of all, Sally and Jim have learned to respect each other's silences and times of withdrawal. They seem to understand the strange estrangement that sometimes invades their lives. They know there are deep places of aloneness in each of them that the other cannot penetrate. They do not resent it. They understand it. They seem to have accepted the basic and inescapable loneliness of existence, and yet in that acceptance, they are comfortable together.

The lives of Jim and Sally are sustained by a deep all-pervading religious faith. They have learned, I suspect, to open their solitude to God, to do the best they know day by day, and to leave the rest to God. They worship together and share the life of the church, understanding that worship is a necessary ingredient in a full life, and that it has something to do with their capacity to cope with themselves and each other.

When we come to the time of "the destruction that wasteth at noonday," when the children all have left home and we are just a little "over the hill" physically and professionally, there are times when we fully understand the mood of Sir Bedivere talking with King Arthur at the end of the saga of the Round Table:

> . . . whither shall I go?

. . . .

> For now I see the true old times are dead,
> When every morning brought a noble chance,
> And every chance brought out a noble knight.

. . . .

> But now the whole Round Table is dissolved
> Which was an image of the mighty world;
> And I, the last, go forth companionless . . .[9]

The world has come full cycle for us. The noble chances of yesterday are only memories and it is too late for many noble hopes to bloom.

There are, however, three things that keep us pushing on together. The first is some dignified work to claim our hands and minds. It may be the old job whose responsibilities we have carried for more years than we care to remember. It may be mediocre and we may be one of the vast number of anonymous workers in a large corporation. Nevertheless, what we do is honorable. It has some meaning in relation to the whole corporation. It is our vocation and even in drudgery and monotony there can be the inner satisfaction of work well done.

Our essential aloneness is tolerable if the labor that commands us is meaningful. Our toil is, or ought to be, more than a means by which we get the things that money can buy. It is the vehicle that enables us to use our God-given gifts and develop the capacities that are ours. It is the means by which we make our contribution to the common good, and it is the altar on which we offer our best to God. It links our lives creatively to the ongoing processes of history. Dignified work, and all toil is dignified, divides the poignancy of our aloneness.

The second vital ingredient of ongoing life is worthy love. In one sense we work for those we love. We toil to provide for our loved ones "in sickness and in health" and love keeps us pushing on through disappointment and frustration. All that we endure of struggle and strain seems small when we feel the gratitude of those for whom we toil. Their reciprocated love is our adequate reward. Loveless labor is a desolate kind of life, solitary beyond measure.

My mind goes back to an evening I spent with a group of men, all of them middle-aged. They met for dinner at their club, and before the evening was far spent, most of them were in their cups. All of them were successful. They were business and professional leaders. Most of them had no wish to hurry home. One man, whose speech was slurred, asked loudly, "Why go home? It's more pleasant here." Quite evidently his home was loveless. Tragically, too, his success was without meaning, and his life was haunted by loneliness.

On the other hand, there are men I know who rejoice to be home. The door to their house or apartment bids them welcome and the warmth of affection embraces them. They meet understanding and appreciation at the dinner table, and they give understanding and gratitude in response. Their aloneness is tempered by the quiet communion of known love and loyalty. They are restored in mind and spirit by the depth of the love they find at home.

Love in middle age is not a matter of "moonlight and roses." It is rather the quiet awareness of each that the other is a source of dependable strength. It is Eve's confidence that no matter what happens Adam will be at her side. It is Adam's sure knowledge that if worse comes to worst, Eve will walk through it with him with steadfast courage. It is the comfortable feeling of security that no other can destroy their life together.

The third sustaining element that keeps us pushing on together is faith in God, the very ground of our being. We find Him in the goodness of our fellowship. We meet Him in the love that enriches our life together. We touch the hem of His garment in moments of shared pain or joy. He comes to us in times of deep communion when, for moments at least, our solitude is broken by a sense of oneness. He invades the hours of our mutual concern for those we love and the times of our caring for neighbors and friends. God is not far off beyond the mists of the Milky Way. He is wherever love and trust are strong and unbreakable, wherever "two or three" are gathered in affection and outgoing concern for others. In pain or suffering we meet His love in the love and compassion of those who care for us. We confront Him in the rejoicing of those who rejoice with us.

Together we make decisions and choices that determine our destiny, and yet, despite our oneness in love and trust, we come to the countdown of hard decision essentially alone.

Countdown Alone

T HE WORD "countdown" was first applied in connection with an atomic explosion at Alamogordo, New Mexico, on July 16, 1945. Some of the scientists who watched that secret explosion almost hoped they were wrong, and that no atomic weapon was possible. Today the word "countdown" is commonplace as we watch rockets blasting off from Cape Kennedy. Throughout the countdown, watching multiple gauges and dials, one man is alone in the valley of decision. Until the final blast-off he waits between "Yes" and "No."

The dominant theme of contemporary life can be expressed in the word "countdown." We are forever in valleys of decision, evaluating circumstances, making up our minds to do or not to do, to go or not to go, to speak out or to remain silent. Edwin Markham in one of his poems posed the issue as if from God Himself:

> I will leave man to make the fateful guess,
> Will leave him torn between No and Yes;
> Leave him in tragic loneliness to choose.
> With all in life to win and all to lose.[1]

The prophet Joel sounded the same note long ago when he wrote from the depths of compassion, "Multitudes, multitudes, in the valley of decision."[2]

ALONE BETWEEN "YES" AND "NO"

Life is a perpetual countdown alone for you and for me. We teeter on the edge of decision, torn between "No" and "Yes," wishing we could know the ending of our ventures before we risk beginning. We even resort to the superstition of horoscopes to guide us. Not long ago somebody with a sense of humor offered two horoscopes for each day. You could take your choice. Under Scorpio, for example, one horoscope said, "Be ready for surprises, quick changes." The other said, "You love to investigate. Put your talent to good use and take your time."

Life always is a choice-making pilgrimage. Daily and hourly we confront the necessity for choice between alternatives. We are a little like the man who was asked by his psychiatrist, "Do you have trouble making up your mind?" The patient replied, "Well, yes and no." Life frequently is impaired by our inability to choose between this and that. We cannot bring the debate between alternatives to a close and decide. That, I suspect, is why Hamlet's soliloquy, "To be or not to be" is the most famous speech in modern literature with an appeal that neither repetition nor parody can destroy. As Houston Peterson noted in *Lonely Debate*, "it [Hamlet's soliloquy] dramatizes for each one of us the baffled individual in the agony of indecision."

Some of life's necessary choices are simple ones, like choosing at a restaurant between boiled salmon and roast beef. There is no use irritating the waiter and everyone else by a long debate before concluding salmon is your choice. At a slightly deeper level, we may have to decide whether to omit mashed potatoes and rolls in the interest of weight control. We have to decide whether we will indulge ourselves or keep a trim figure. Deeper yet, we may be confronted by a choice between *filet mignon* and ground beef. If we have ground beef we can give two dollars to some worthy cause. If we eat *filet mignon,* we cannot.

Every choice we make involves a series of relationships and consequences. The young man trying to find his place in the world, has to decide to stay in the bank where he is employed, do his best and wait for a promotion, or to leave the bank and try something else in pastures that look greener. He has to decide in the isolation of his own soul whether he is too impatient or whether his situation is a dead-end street. He has to make up his mind whether he has what it takes to be an effective and competent banker or whether he is better fitted to be something else.

In Macaulay's description of Lord Clive on the eve of the battle of Plassey there is a striking instance of the burden and loneliness of difficult decision. Before Clive lay a river over which it would have been easy to advance, but if things went wrong "not one of his little band would return." His troops were vastly outnumbered by the enemy and most of his officers opposed advance. Clive agreed. He retired under the shade of some trees "and passed nearly an hour there in thought. He came back determined to put everything to the hazard, and gave orders that all should be in readiness for passing the river on the morrow."[3]

The river was crossed and Clive's small forces won a decisive victory. The hour of decision was a terrifyingly lonely one, but it was decisive in its consequences. Many millions of British and Indian people were affected by it. But Clive necessarily walked alone choosing between "Yes" and "No." So all of us are essentially isolated in ourselves when we choose between alternatives.

Decision often is difficult, especially when we face unattractive possibilities no matter what we do. There are times when we are disposed to feel that no matter which road we take we probably will wish we had taken the other. The quarterback with four yards to go and confronted by a line of two-hundred pounders who will not yield, and a couple of his own ends who cannot seem to hang onto the ball, has to decide whether to run or pass. Whichever choice he makes, he probably will wish he had made the other.

If the quarterback takes too much time making up his mind, his team is penalized five yards. The penalties we suffer for indecision are less obvious, but no less real. Life moves on whether we decide or fail to decide what to do when crowded by circumstances requiring a choice. Herman Melville noted the fatal disposition of multitudes who "sail around an island without landing, and talk around a subject without getting at it," and Samuel Johnson despaired of men and women who arrive at conclusions in which "nothing is concluded."

Haunted and troubled we wander in the valley of decision, torn between "No" and "Yes," and we are incredibly anxious and lonely. We wish someone would decide for us and relieve the strain. I smiled a little while ago when I saw an advertisement for an "Executive Decision Maker," a silver dollar mounted on a marble base and attached in a frame so that it could be turned over and over. Underneath were the words, "Decisions, decisions, decisions add up to tension. You may ease tension by spinning this dollar while you are making up your mind via its 'Heads-you-don't-and-tails-you-do.' "

It should be noted, however, that neither horoscopes nor spinning dollars constitute a dependable base for decision-making in any area of our experience. Decisions are intimately personal and there always is an essential aloneness in the "valley of decision." To leave decision in the hands of others, or to the words of a horoscope, or to the flip of a coin is to do violence to our own essential freedom and to deny the deeps of personal responsibility.

To be sure, important decisions deserve to be considered seriously, but sooner or later we had better cease going around the island and land somewhere. There comes a time when all the available evidence is in and the only reason for not resolving the issue is irresolution.

THE CHALLENGE OF DECISION-MAKING

There is an old Chinese proverb to the effect that "The longest journey begins with but a single step." So it is that the journey to our destiny begins with a single choice, a single step one way or another when we are in the valley of decision. On the Mount of Temptation Jesus met the issues of His life alone, issues dramatically detailed to be sure, and yet the same issues you and I confront in our lonely valleys. He set the course of His life and took a single giant step toward His destiny.

Life assumes a positive, creative aspect when in the presence of issues we decide to decide. Not to decide often is fatal. When it comes to important decisions there are four things to remember. The first is that nobody expects you to be infallible. As Cromwell noted, "Remember, by the love of Christ, that you may be mistaken." Every choice you make has within it the possibility of error. You can be wrong no matter how carefully you observe the alternatives. But a mistake is not necessarily fatal if you give the issue the honest thought it deserves. You will make more mistakes wandering in the wilderness of indecision than you will in making occasional wrong choices. Lord Nelson noted wisely that "The boldest measures are the safest," and in the long run that is true.

The second comment is the reminder that problems, as Regina Wieman noted, "keep us from settling into stagnant pools. They swirl us into the deeper currents of real living and make us reach out for the life-line of life."[4] It is through dealing creatively with truculent problems that growth and maturity take place. We may wish decisions would not crowd us into lonely corners as they do, and yet the issues that must be met stab us awake and thrust us "into the deeper currents of real living." If we are alive we are grateful for the challenge of problems to be solved.

The third thing to remember is that most wrong decisions can be remedied when the mistake has been discovered. Once I asked Charles Francis Berry, a major league umpire, if he ever made mistakes in calling balls and strikes. He looked at me as if he thought I had asked a moronic question. Then he said, "Of course I make mistakes. My only trouble is I can't admit it." Our hope in life is the humility to admit to ourselves and others that, not being infallible, we have made a mistake. And confessed mistakes normally can be remedied.

The fourth observation is that we never know whether or not we have made a wrong decision until the dye is cast. There is a suggestion of the truth in a scene from one of the old silent serial films. The hero of the cast was fleeing from the villains of the plot, pushing his way through a forest, with a raging forest fire behind him. He comes at last to a chasm, dropping out of sight in front of him. The other side of the chasm is ten feet away. He never has jumped ten feet before, and he does not know whether he can make the leap successfully. But with the flames and the villains behind him he has no choice but to try.

Just what happened to my hero I shall never know. Poised on the brink of the chasm, with the audience breathless, the weekly episode came to an end with the words, "To be continued next week." The next Saturday afternoon I had to mow the lawn so I never learned what happened to the hero of the plot. But in any event, the man about to leap the chasm could not know whether or not he was wise to jump until he jumped. It is so in life.

Usually the issues we meet in our lives are not as hazardous as that of the hero of the silent movie. Errors of judgment, admitted, usually can be rectified before irreparable damage has been done. The only fatal error is to press on with a wrong choice, refusing to confess it or take measures to rectify it.

GROUNDS OF CHOOSING

Of course, we do not need to make as many mistakes as we do. We can evaluate the evidence more carefully and make our choices in relation to abiding standards to which we have committed ourselves. There are clear-cut choices between right and wrong that need occasion no debate. Plainly, it never is wrong to do right. When life has been committed to God half the issues of life are resolved without debate, and in the presence of alternatives the course is clear. We can do no other.

On the other hand, there are many decisions in which we have no sharply defined choice between black and white. In an election, for example, we may have the choice of voting for a gin-guzzling politician who has a reasonably good voting record and a reactionary conservative who still is fighting the battles that were lost in 1912. The choice between the two is not of world-shaking ethical consequence. Of course, there was an available prior choice, namely, to toil or not to toil at the precinct level and in the community, to effect the nomination of political candidates of intellectual and moral stature so that voting finally has ethical impact. There is, as Brooke Herford noted, "a small end to great problems." The trouble is we seldom take hold of the small end.

One of the most striking illustrations of the truth was suggested by the comment of Archbishop Temple at the time of the abdication of Edward VIII of Great Britain. Edward had to choose between a woman and his duty to the nation. Dr. Temple observed, "The occasion for Edward's choice ought never to have arisen. It has happened to many a man before now to find himself falling in love with another man's wife. That is the moment of critical decision, and the right decision is that they should cease to meet before passion is so developed as to create an agonizing conflict between love and duty."

There is a small and manageable handle to every issue of our common life, but too often we wait until the small handle has vanished. What often happens was strikingly illustrated at the Republican National Convention of 1964. One faction of the party took hold of the small handle of the issue, working for four years, precinct by precinct, county by county, and state by state. The other faction waited and did little until its problem had become unmanageable. The issue was decided before the convention began. Thereafter there were agonizing and unhappy choices to be made that left the party a shambles.

Some time ago I visited with a man who is an alcoholic. A few years ago there was a small handle to his problem. He knew he was asking for trouble, going overboard now and then, drinking too much with his friends. But he could not decide to say "No" until it was too late. He went down to the bottom before he began to make a recovery, one that was agony all the way. He did not understand that every day was judgment day.

The former governor of Oklahoma, the popular Raymond Gary, was asked "What is the hardest task a governor has?" He answered simply, "Saying 'No.' " And "Saying 'No' " often is the small end of what may become an unmanageable problem.

It was Professor H. N. Wieman who noted there are as many ways of taking hold of issues as there are of taking hold of a cat. We can seize the legs, the tail or the nape of the neck; all are equally part of the cat. If we grab the tail or the legs, we have not missed the cat; we truly have it. But the consequences often are disastrous and at best uncertain, since it is not a very useful way to take hold of a cat. We learn promptly that we had better take the cat by the nape of the neck if we want to do anything with it. That is the small handle to a scratching cat.

CONFLICTING LOYALTIES

The cultural patterns of contemporary life complicate the decision-making processes. As Martin Marty says, we are living in a "post-Christian era." The traditional values of our heritage have largely given way to an age of wistfulness. In practice we ignore the virtues of our heritage, and yet we are wistful for them. Like Leonardo da Vinci in his confused time, we wonder: "What has happened to our concepts of beauty, decency and morality?"

It is a large question to which there is no complete answer. Certainly the liberties permitted on stage and screen, the lack of integrity in our common life, and the disturbing obscenity in books and magazines suggest the absence of shame in our society. At any rate, being Christian in our contemporary society is a lonely chore for heroes only. The charge committed to us is no easy one. A Japanese writer in a Tokyo magazine divides us in the United States into two classes: "Obliques" and "Straights." Makuto Oda explains that "straight" America is represented by those who stress the nation's traditional values. But "oblique" America, says Mr. Oda with approval, "is an America that doubts and compromises and looks backward as well as forward."

The definitions are a little fuzzy, but the Merriam-Webster dictionary is more helpful. "Straight" means "Keeping true to a correct course or method; . . . candid; frank. . . . Conforming to justice and rectitude; upright." "Oblique," on the other hand, can be defined as "Not straightforward; evasive; hence, disingenuous; underhand." The dictionary ends the definition with: "Syn. See 'crooked.'" Perhaps the indictment was not intended as an indictment. The author thoroughly approves of "oblique" America, and that is the troubling aspect of the matter. We do seem to approve of "oblique" behavior and, therefore, the Christian finds himself pushing against the tide.

We use various yardsticks when we are confronted by choices between alternatives that are neither all black nor all white. We may keep our eyes on our interests, our social class, our political party, our business, and so on. Arthur Koestler's novel of Stalinist Russia, *Darkness at Noon*, unflinchingly faces many of the dilemmas which follow from Lenin's theory of the Party, and no scene is more poignant than that between the old party stalwart, Rubashov, and the youthful rebel, Richard. "The Party never can be mistaken," said Rubashov. "You and I can make a mistake. Not the Party. The Party, comrade, is more than you and I and a thousand others like you and I. He who has not absolute faith . . . does not belong in the Party's ranks."[5]

In Richard, however, there was gnawing doubt, as if somehow there ought to be room for the right of private judgment. He could not rid his mind of disturbing concepts of truth and justice, goodness and love which, he knew, had no place in the counsels of the Party. He was torn between loyalty and integrity and his lonely dilemma was a searing and a torturing one.

Often our dilemmas center in conflicting loyalties. It is not a question of being faithful to love, to duty, to vows, to obligations. The problem goes deeper, namely, to how do we deal with conflicting loyalties? Is one loyalty more ultimate than another? Naaman, the Syrian, cleansed of his leprosy, swore that he would be loyal to the God of Israel, but he promptly realized that when he went back to Syria he would have to go with his master into the temple of Rimmon and in loyalty to his master, bow down before Rimmon. Naaman was deeply torn between his loyalty to the God of Israel and his devotion to his monarch, the King of Syria. "Bowing down in the house of Rimmon" has become a proverb suggesting the danger of compromise.

Our conflict of loyalties may be very real when we choose between alternatives in an "oblique" society. Love may be in conflict with duty, and loyalty in conflict with obligation, but nine times out of ten we are able to discern what is more right than wrong if we love God with our minds as well as with our hearts.

The letters of Robert E. Lee are both tragic and poignant because they reveal the conflict in him between loyalty to the United States and love for the State of Virginia. His inner struggle was a searing one before he finally cast his lot with Virginia. In the light of history, his judgment was fallible. He never really faced the crucial issue as crucial, namely, man's enslavement of his fellow men. Like most of us, he made his choice between loyalty and love without seeing that justice and the dignity of all mankind were also involved. He fought gallantly and with a good conscience because he was able to obscure the basic issue.

More often than not our human conflicts rage because in good conscience we are wrong, thinking we are right. We forget that when we are "under God" we are obliged to think through issues until we have plumbed beneath the surface to ultimate values. Prejudices and biased opinions cannot stand the judgment of God and leave us in the end with a good conscience. We can go wrong thinking we are right only when we are able to keep God at arm's length and obscure basic issues.

Nobody is more difficult than the man or woman who is sincerely wrong. He thinks he is serving the good when in reality he is struggling against God. He identifies his opinions or prejudices with the will of God and he is like a stampeding herd, hard to turn from his course.

"The judgments of God are true and righteous altogether," while our judgments are fallible. So, our dilemmas are disturbing, but if we face them as disciples of our Lord, with humility, honesty, and selflessness, seeking the will of God for our lives, we most certainly will be more right than wrong.

HOLDING FAITH

In Paul's letter to Timothy he suggested there was no alternative to "holding faith" in something ultimate. John Gunther put the issue in perspective when he wrote that whenever he goes to a foreign country and visits the head of the state he tries to discover the answer to two questions: first, what are the real sources of power behind the man? Second, what does he believe in most?

In the area of either personal or political life what a man believes in most is decisive. Woodrow Wilson, for example, once broke with a powerful politician and bluntly refused to play politics with the good of the nation. He was accused of ingratitude. His decision was a difficult one after his nomination for president. It might have cost him needed votes in the election to come. But, as one editorial of the day observed, "It passes our understanding that a candidate for president . . . can be assailed for having the conscience to speak God's truth."

As for the charge of ingratitude, the New York *World* disposed of the matter in an editorial widely quoted. "Ingratitude," said the editorial, "is one of the rarest virtues in public life. 'Gratitude' is responsible for many of our political abuses. Upon 'gratitude' is founded the power of every ignorant and unscrupulous boss; in 'gratitude' is rooted the system of spoils, of logrolling, of lobbying." The editorial concluded, "No, what we need in public life is a great deal more discriminating ingratitude."[6]

Woodrow Wilson, as he made clear repeatedly, believed most in God, and his conscience responded to his most ultimate loyalty in a crisis. He turned his back on the spoils system and on the habit of rewarding political hacks to the detriment of the nation. So, John Gunther, acute reporter that he is, sensed that the fate of men and nations depends on the ultimate beliefs of men.

There is a further illustration, in a negative way, of the same truth in a disturbing book by Anthony Sampson, an able and cultured journalist. Sampson studied the centers of power in English life, the court, the cabinet, parliament, the civil service, the church, the armed services, the law, the city, big business, the trade unions, TV, radio, and so on. He painted a terrifying picture of unco-ordinated drift in which many who hold levers of power, as well as men and women of average status, are either thwarted by others or are carried along by currents outside their control to goals of which they are only partially aware. Mr. Sampson called his investigation a "baffling journey," and the two epigraphs to his last chapter are significant. One is the comment of Barbara Wootton, "Everything is always decided somewhere else." The other is from a poem by W. B. Yeats, called "The SecondComing." It reads:

> Things fall apart; the center cannot hold,
> Mere anarchy is loosed upon the world.[7]

These quotations are commentary on the observation of an English cabinet minister who said, "The trouble is, we don't believe in anything."

If we were to study the anatomy of the United States, I dare say we would find a similar lostness brooding over our common life, with ample evidence of ethical and spiritual muddling. We, no less than the British, are adrift. We do not believe in anything very much. The Ten Commandments are honored more in the breach than in the observance. The Beatitudes, as J. B. Phillips suggests, have been revised to read,

> Happy are the pushers: for they get on in the world.
> Happy are the hard-boiled: for they never let life hurt them.
> Happy are they who complain: for they get their own way in the end.
> Happy are the blasé: for they never worry over their sins.
> Happy are the trouble-makers: for they make people take notice
> of them.[8]

So we might go on with the Beatitudes of our contemporary world.

We seem to be living on the assumption that so long as nothing terribly bad is happening to us we need not worry. However, if we are to survive and create a world worthy of our children, we are constrained to create a society in which something positively good is happening. It is not enough to have a breather between crises. The problem is so to think and serve that crises result in progress.

In what are we really "holding faith," if in anything? The question is decisive. It is ultimate, for example, for one who sits as a judge in a court of law faced with the necessity of making extremely difficult decisions. His decisions necessarily are determined by what he believes in most. That was true of the distinguished Christian jurist, Augustus N. Hand. One who knew him said that those who watched him at work "gained new insight and courage." They discovered that "beyond the clash of interests and the compromise of competing claims there can be found standards of rectitude and generosity and that in the search for these standards and in the steadfast adherence to them lies the triumph of man."

Archibald MacLeish wrote in tribute to Judge Hand:

> We are neither weak nor few.
> As long as one man does what one can do—
> As long as one man in the sun alone
> Walks between the silence and the stone
> And honors manhood in his flesh, his bone,
> We are not yet too weak, nor yet too few.[9]

It is so!

When one man believes in God more than in all else, he stands in the lonely grandeur of independent integrity guided by the light of "standards of rectitude and generosity." He may make errors of judgment because he is a fallible being in an "oblique" society, but over the long run he will be more right than wrong. "As long as one man does what one can do" with integrity of spirit and in loyalty to God there is hope.

A SPIRITUAL FRAMEWORK

Our task, therefore, is to keep the issues of our lives in a spiritual framework. The choices we make always are subject to the final judgment of God, and there is no use coming to the end of the road feeling as Napoleon did that "There seems to have been some misunderstanding between me and God." There need be no great misunderstanding between God and ourselves if our choices and decisions are made within a spiritual framework.

Our faith in God is revealed in our critical intelligence choosing among alternatives in the light of the abiding standards. A primitive admonition is contained in the wisdom literature of the Hebrews:

> Remove not the ancient landmark,
> Which thy fathers have set.[10]

Our faith in the Jesus of history provides dependable landmarks for thought and action. In the light of His mind, there are choices and decisions that are outside the possible. We cannot destroy another to save ourselves. We cannot embark on a course whose end is the violation of our integrity. We cannot undertake a venture designed to leave our fellow men poorer in spirit and mind. The ancient landmark is clear.

It was Karl Barth who noted that God injects into human life an absolute crisis. In every concrete decision each individual faces the ultimate choice of his life. The choice is the necessity for deciding for or against God. The crisis does not arise only once, but in every case where a decision must be made. As Emerson noted, "Every day is doomsday" because each day's decisions bear upon the whole direction of life.

No doubt, whatever I do will be deeply infected with evil

simply because all of life is enmeshed in the evils of this world. Nevertheless, I decide for God when "every interest of mine, every value, every hope and ideal and course of action is held by me as subject to judgment" under God.

If I decide for God I am released from fears and passions, envies, prejudices, and obsessions that twist my judgment. I am under the mastery of God. Of course, none of my decisions can claim to be wholly God's way, for "our ways" never are altogether "His ways," and "our thoughts" never are fully "His thoughts." Nevertheless, I can examine all the possibilities of every decision on their merits, not enslaved to the lure or the fear of any.

John Baillie was correct when he said that "In moments of moral choice we have our deepest dealings with the universe."[11] In all our choices between good and evil, better and best, we have significant dealings with God. Jesus made that clear on the Mount of Temptation. In His choices there He was not operating in a vacuum. On the contrary He was involved with the deepest values in the structure of the universe. He was dealing with God, with God's will and purpose, and so are we all when we walk alone in the "valley of decision."

Every decision we make, in one way or another, involves our total relationship to the universe. If I choose deception, my choice puts me at odds with the God of things as they are. If I decide to be silent when I ought to speak in the name of justice, my choice leaves me pushing against the grain of the universe. In my choices between good will and vindictiveness, between sacrifice and selfishness, I have my most urgent dealings with God. My decisions are not isolated from the values that are rooted in the nature of God's economy.

There is a stirring illustration of the mood which lies at the heart of the Christian faith in K. C. Wu's *The Lane of Eternal Stability*, the story of the Communist conquest of China. One episode is particularly relevant. Li Chien, the Communist, insisted that Yuwen saw "a moral everywhere." Ta-kong, leaning in the Communist direction, tried to make peace between Yuwen, the Christian, and Li Chien, the Communist. "As I see it," he said, "there's no real difference between your views. The practice of deceit and craft, when considered independently, must be unequivocally condemned." But "in real life if one wants to achieve a big ideal he must be prepared to sacrifice some small ones."[12]

But Yuwen stuck to his ground. "I beg to differ," he said. "What is idealism but a compound of ideals? How can there be a big ideal unless it's supported by lesser ones? Idealism is whole and indivisible."[13] And so it is. The ultimate values of human experience compose a whole that is indivisible. There is no such thing as a minor violation of a major value because all ultimate values, love and truth, justice and integrity are rooted in the very nature of God.

So, in our aloneness, making value judgments and choices we have our clearest commerce with God. Every decision we make touching the lives of others involves God because God cares for persons. Every choice we make between deception and integrity involves God because God is truth, the whole truth. However much we try, we cannot escape God.

The reality of our inescapable God, whose goodness endures beyond the shadows of time or tide, leads us to feelings of guilt and shame however much we seek to deceive ourselves. Often we are wistful, lonely, and afraid because we feel we are guilty outsiders.

6

Guilty Outsider

THE STRAIN of living under the pressures of the contemporary world intensifies our need for inner tranquility. As Axel Munthe wrote, "A man can stand a lot as long as he can stand himself."[1] In no area of our experience is the "inscape" more significant than in the area of guilt. We can live through the worst life can do to us if we are able to live with our memories, if we are able to listen to our own thoughts.

Our answer to the question, "What's on your mind?" determines in large measure whether or not we can endure loneliness and bear the strain of outward things. If our sleep is haunted by the ghosts of unforgiven sins, the stress of life may well be more than we can bear. If we cannot stand ourselves, we cannot stand. If we cannot endure the guilt we feel, neither can we endure the strain of our aloneness. That much is growing clearer day by day.

Leslie Weatherhead, after years of counseling at City Temple, London, noted that more neuroses come from repressed guilt than from anything else. We know that broken men and women are everywhere, filling hospital beds and mental institutions to the brim, and many of them are where they are because they cannot stand themselves. Still more are "walking shadows," living without zest, plodding through weary days, drowning their sorrows at night or rushing hither and yon in a vain effort not to think. Because they cannot stand themselves they are trying desperately to run away from themselves. It is a futile business.

The truth is that when we betray the confidence of others, or make a shambles of the highest and the best we know, a sense of shame and guilt breaks through the stoutest bulwarks we can build with excuses and alibis. We are tortured by the lonely tempest in the inner man. Do not tell me it cannot make you ill, upset your digestion, and lay you low with palsied fear. I have seen and known too many men and women broken by the guilts that festered in their minds. Like Cain, the murderer, they came to the place where they knew in bitterness, "My punishment is greater than I can bear."[2]

The alcoholic knows the truth. Usually, for all his bluster, he is acutely sensitive to right and wrong. Nine times out of ten he is a man who hates himself the way he is. His sins, multiplied in his inebriation, become morning-after guilt. He cannot stand himself when he is sober, so he seeks at least temporary escape in another spree. He is caught on an endless wheel of sin followed by guilt from which he cannot seem to escape. Medical cures are feeble reeds because they do not touch the deepest sickness of the spirit.

Most of us are like the alcoholic except for the fact that we, being less sensitive, less high-strung than he, devise other means for dealing with our guilt. If we can manage it, we use what Nietzsche called "the hidden lie." We do one of three things. We deceive ourselves with alibis that put the blame on someone else. The game is as old as Adam blaming Eve and Eve pointing to the serpent in the Garden of Eden. Or, perhaps, we dress our sins in garments of virtue and convince ourselves we did the only thing we could "under the circumstances" and "considering everything." Or, it may be that like the intellectuals of the "lost generation" we excuse our sins by sneering at our aspirations. We were sentimental fools to cherish impossible ideals!

The difficulty is that sooner or later "the hidden lie" which sustains our self-deceptions turns out to be a lie. It will not bear the burden of time or life. Like the little grebes, similar to loons, who are carried on the backs of their mothers, only to have their mothers forget them and duck under, we trust in the hidden lie only to have it duck under and leave us bobbing in the eddies. It dives under when we least expect it and it leaves us reeling. Possibly we blunder into someone whose character shames us with evidence of what life can be. Maybe, like Augustine, we blunder into Jesus Christ and find ourselves defenseless. When the "hidden lie" ducks under we are swamped by our sense of guilt.

ALIENATING GUILT

The consequence of guilt is isolation. Comradeship is thwarted by an inner block. We are fearful lest we reveal ourselves for what we really are. The deep communion of understanding is inhibited by "the hidden lie" that defies all probing. We keep our friends and loved ones at arm's length lest the private sin become more public than we wish. We are guilty outsiders, fearful of confession, more fearful of exposure.

One man, whose marriage went on the rocks, and whose outward self-assurance was shattered by the shock, poured out the sordid story of his past as if he had to get it out. "I've lived a lie for twenty years," he said, "and never dared to look at myself." An extrovert, he had managed to appear the soul of honor, and to win a place of respect in the community. But his world fell apart in his hands and his sense of guilt overwhelmed him. He felt like an alien in the world that once had been his bowl of cherries.

O. Hobart Mowrer put the truth in perspective when he wrote, "Over the years it has been my growing conviction that the thing that most severely damages our capacity to love and to be lovable is not neglect or rejection by others, but unacknowledged and unatoned personal guilt."[3] On the other hand, "the strongest incentive for brotherly love (and, actually, for sexual love as well) is a clear conscience."[4] Guilt imposes alienation; a clear conscience opens doors to fellowship.

Even when the sin is secret, conscience finds us, imposing alienation on us. Our isolation is self-imposed. The fact that sin has made possible the ill-gotten gains we sought does not help. So King Claudius found in Shakespeare's *Hamlet:*

> . . . But, O! what form of prayer
> Can serve my turn? "Forgive me my foul murder"?

> That cannot be; since I am still possess'd
> Of those effects for which I did the murder—
> My crown, mine own ambition, and my queen.[5]

The haunting inner tumult in Claudius left him on edge, uneasy in the company of those who knew nothing of his guilt. There was, too, a deeper isolation of the spirit, and Claudius wondered,

> May one be pardon'd and retain th' offence?
> In the corrupted currents of this world
> Offence's gilded hand may shove by justice,
> And oft 'tis seen the wicked prize itself
> Buys out the law: but 'tis not so above.
> There is no shuffling, there the action lies
> In his true nature; and we ourselves compell'd
> Even to the teeth and forehead of our faults,
> To give in evidence.[6]

There is a similar note in O. Henry's story of the thief who sat one evening smoking a big cigar in the park. He had swindled a child out of a dollar for breakfast, and tricked a simple-hearted old man out of a wad of notes for dinner. His eyes were fat and sparkling until the clock struck nine and he saw a young woman hurrying home. She was dressed in simple white. Years ago he had known her. He had sat on the same bench with her at school. And suddenly he got up and turned down a side street and laid his burning face against the cool iron of a lamp post and said dully, "God, I wish I could die."

Nothing separated the thief from the woman in white except the sin in his own heart and mind. Nothing separated Claudius from the companionship of those who composed his court save the tortured thoughts he could not brush away. What is more, nothing separated either the thief or Claudius from the love of God except the inner guilt of honor and loyalty defied.

Sin is like driving the wrong way on a one-way street. Even though the street is deserted we feel as if a thousand hostile eyes were on us. We are at odds with the proper flow of things, pushing against a required tide. We may bluster and complain the signs were not clear, but we feel the wrongness of our going, our separation from the motorists traveling as they ought. If we persist in going the wrong way on a one-way street, we invite disaster and even sudden death.

Eugene O'Neill, who helped to bring American drama to maturity, revealed the deep inner conflicts of his characters, conflicts that brought on them personal tragedy and disaster. He was aware of the agony of inner guilt. He pictured the truth in one of his most provocative plays, *The Iceman Cometh*. In one episode of the play Hickey, the drunken salesman, whose cronies all were alcoholics, described the way his wife forgave him time and again when he came home after a spree, with a hang-over and even with evidences of infidelity. Despite his sordid ways she loved him still. "Can you imagine what a guilty skunk she made me feel?" Hickey asked his companions. "I hated myself."[7]

Unhappily, Hickey preferred his self-hatred to reformation. He might have been redeemed by love and forgiveness, but he rejected both, and as a consequence his self-hate was intensified until it became unbearable. As he saw the matter, he had only one of two choices: he could murder his wife or he could change his ways. He murdered his wife.

Hickey's dilemma is a parable of the spiritual life. When we are burdened by feelings of guilt and self-hatred we have one of two choices, the same choices that confronted those who sent Jesus to the cross. We can respond creatively to love and forgiveness and be reconciled to God, or we can crucify Him by rejection. Like Augustine and a multitude of others we can accept the forgiveness of God and move off in new directions, or, like Jean-Paul Sartre, we can blot God out of the picture and blunder toward what he calls "nothingness" from which there is "no exit."

Going the wrong way on a one-way street is an enterprise for fools only. The wise repent, like the Prodigal Son, and turn around to go the other way, seeking forgiveness and "newness of life." Unhappily, there are too many fools on the road who push on against the spiritual traffic of the universe.

Years ago a friend of mine, on the edge of a nervous breakdown, went to a psychiatrist for help. Jim's father was a retired minister, a grand old gentleman. When his father retired, Jim bought a home for his father and mother a few doors from his own home. But Jim, a sudden success in business, was traveling in newly discovered fast company. He was drinking too much and pretending to be uninhibited. The psychiatrist put his finger on Jim's trouble. Jim's father, living so near, was a symbol of everything his son was trying to ignore. He stood as an unrelenting prophet of God, even though he wisely kept his own counsel and said nothing in criticism of his son. The psychiatrist gave my friend a bit of sound advice. There were two possible courses of action. Either he could reorganize his life and change his company, or else he could give up going to church and send his father to some other town. He could not go on as he was, perpetually reminded that he ought to be something else.

Jim thought the matter through and decided to give up the church and send his father somewhere else. He did just that. He thought he could eliminate his sense of guilt by getting rid of the things that reminded him of it. He avoided a nervous breakdown for a time, but life for him remained a burden and a regret. He found no joy in living, for he had cut off his spiritual oxygen supply and was on the verge of spiritual suffocation. The radiant good will that once had made him loved and admired turned into a somber bitterness that left him lonely. Trying to go the wrong way on a one-way street, he met disaster, the disaster of isolation and alienation from both man and God.

THE SENSE OF SIN

Relieving the strain of guilt begins, of course, in admitting that our sin is sin. Even the holiest of men always have prayed with Wordsworth,

> The best of what we do and are
> Just God forgive.[8]

"Clear Thou me from hidden faults,"[9] is the prayer of the spiritually mature. Not one of us is good enough, as I John notes, "If we say we have no sin, we deceive ourselves."[10] We may wish to avoid the truth, but we have unreasoned prejudices. We are selfish. We often are proud and condescending. We have impure thoughts. We do not always speak "the truth, the whole truth, and nothing but the truth." We are loveless at times and cantankerous, too. Clearly, "if we say we have no sin, we decieve ourselves." We had better be honest about the matter.

Unhappily, modern man has a way of looking on the "sense of sin" as a bit of unmeaning theological jargon. There is, however, another kind of talk he understands, namely, that of the new psychology. He understands, for example, the phrase "inferiority complex." Possibly moderns would understand the "sense of sin" if it were called a moral inferiority complex. At any rate, there are multitudes who feel an uneasy dissatisfaction with themselves. Their protective pride keeps them from admitting that their sin is sin. Reinhold Niebuhr notes that under the "perpetual smile of modernity" there is "a grimace of disillusion and cynicism." Quite possibly the grimace is indicative of a "moral inferiority complex," unconfessed and unacknowledged, but there nevertheless.

Psychologists tell us that a neurosis often develops when we make a mistake and then protect the mistake with a lie. Obviously, not all mistakes lead to neurotic difficulties or all of us would be in the hands of psychiatrists. There are those who "get caught" and others who voluntarily confess and take the consequences. On the other hand, there are some who do not get caught and do not confess. They defend their mistake, or sin, with a lie to themselves and others. Nevertheless, their emotions are involved. Psychological difficulty may be postponed while they try to overcome their moral inferiority complex with alibis and rationalizations, but in due time the period of grace expires and conscience becomes an unbearable critic. Then the neurosis develops, and with it isolation and alienation.

It is significant to notice that mental illness has defied our best efforts to cope with it, or even to understand it. At the same time the acids of modernity have led us to an increasing disparagement of ethical values. Is it possible that there is a vital connection between the two? The "hidden lie" may well be the ultimate root of mental illness, and the "grimace of disillusion and cynicism" the retribution of unacknowledged moral inferiority.

Jack London tried to overcome his moral inferiority complex

with relentless bluster, but at psychotic cost. Like Buck, the California dog, in *The Call of the Wild,* London suppressed the more sensitive side of his nature in his effort to beat the magazines and, as Van Wyck Brooks observed, "get up in a world in which you did not prosper if you had scruples." London noted that "morality is only an evidence of low blood pressure,"[11] and then went on to behave as if he believed it. However, he could not beat the deck. It was stacked against him.

Unless we are honest enough to confess that sin is sin and no rationalization can make it anything else, we are bound to get splinters pushing against the grain of the universe. The splinters may come in the form of neuroses, cynicism and bitterness, a sense of the futility of life, or boredom. Most painful, however, they come in the form of loneliness and alienation.

Young people today, like the youth of every generation, find themselves in tension, torn between loyalty to the virtues held to be important in their homes and churches and the collegiate drive for moral freedom and experimentation. Rebellion is afoot among those of the rising generation. My generation was rebellious, too. Headlines described us as "flaming youth." Clara Bow, the "It" girl, and Rudolph Valentino, the "Sheik," were the equivalent of Elizabeth Taylor and Richard Burton now. They shocked our elders and delighted us in our immaturity.

My generation practiced hypocrisy in reverse. We were intent on giving the impression we were worse than we were. Underneath, we were idealists, but we hated to admit it. We wanted to be at least reasonably good, but not too good. We pretended to a sophistication we did not feel inside.

Dennis the Menace, for all his humorous antics, often sounds a solid note. Dennis appeared in a cartoon form kneeling at his bedside, in trouble as usual. He prayed, perhaps with one eye on his mother who was standing by, "An' if ya can't make me a good boy, can ya fix it so Mom won't care?" Dennis rated "A" for effort on two counts: first, he wanted to be better than he was and, second, he wished to avoid upsetting his mother.

Today's young people on the whole are much like Dennis. They would like to be better than they are. However, their dilemma often is acute. On the one hand, they wish to please their parents and on the other they are eager to be accepted by their age group. The two drives often are incompatible. I vividly recall the time in grade school when I was put into a class with the slow learners. My mother, in great distress, hurried to see my teacher. She departed from the interview in tears. My feelings were somewhat mixed. On the one hand, I was delighted. I was precisely where I wanted to be, with my gang. If I had been in the upper class I would have been a traitor to my crowd. On the other hand, I was troubled because my mother was upset.

In retrospect it seems clear that at the time and under the circumstances I preferred the approval of the group to the approval of my parents. Nevertheless, I was uneasy, aware of inner conflict from which I could not escape. My sense of guilt was intensified by the fact that the motto of our Sunday School class was, "Study to shew thyself approved unto God, a workman that needeth not to be ashamed,"[12] and Mr. Winchester, the teacher, had a way of emphasizing the motto at the conclusion of each class session. I resolved my conflict after a fashion by being at the top of the backward class.

A considerable number of young people today are trying to resolve their conflicts in similar fashion, by being at the top of the backward class in more ways than one. They would like to be good, but not too good, and bad, but not too bad; good enough to avoid real trouble and bad enough to fit into their group.

Young people find it difficult to be honest about sin, even though they feel uncomfortable about their behavior. They rationalize wrong by insisting, "Everybody's doing it." "It's a pretty well-known fact," said a Radcliffe College sophomore, "that sex goes on in every college." But, as the *Wall Street Journal* noted, "The young lady got her tenses mixed. Sex not only goes on; it always has went. It is only youthfulness that makes the young think they have discovered something new."[13] The young lady's remark was intended as an argument for more permissive rules on dating in college dormitory rooms.

The Ten Commandments and the Sermon on the Mount have not been nullified for the benefit of the rising generation. Sin remains sin and continues to exact its price in guilt and shame. It goes on, as it always has, leaving emotional disturbances, fears, anxieties, and lonely regret in its wake. As a college roommate of mine used to say, "Imagination of evil is bad enough; memory would be infinitely worse."

FALSE GUILT

We need to be honest, too, about the fact that society has thrust guilt feelings on us that have nothing to do with sin. Guilt feelings are pushed into consciousness by an activist culture. We who are caught up in the patterns of pressure business sometimes feel guilty if we are not constantly pressing, everlastingly at work. There is a striking illustration of the hazard in Sloan Wilson's *Man in the Gray Flannel Suit,* in the gnawing sense of guilt that troubled Tom. The author notes sensitively that

Hopkins rarely left his office before seven o'clock, and Tom sensed he was annoyed to find that Tom usually left earlier. It was embarrassing to have to compete with Hopkins' hours—it was like taking a Sunday afternoon walk with a long-distance runner. The stereotyped notion of the earnest young man arriving early and leaving late, and the complacent boss dropping in for a few hours in the middle of the day to see how things were going was completely reversed.[14]

Tom's sense of embarrassment and guilt were unjustified and painfully out of proportion. The sin lay elsewhere, in Hopkins' disposition to make Tom feel guilty.

There is no virtue in wearing ourselves thin for the "good old company" at the expense of our homes and our families. To be sure, we are constrained to give ourselves to "whatever our hands find to do" with all our might, but there are limits, and none has the right to impose a sense of guilt on another when the limits have been reached. Tom was quite right in recognizing there are values more ultimate than status in business.

Young executives today are more likely to err with Hopkins and to give too much to business and too little to their homes. If they are married to their businesses they often lose the values that make their business progress worth the cost. If they sacrifice the peace of their homes and the comradeship of their children their guilt is deep and their unremitting toil is a "vain striving after the wind." They need to be honest in their appraisal of the values they seek in life.

There is, then, another need for honesty in the approach that women make to their homes. Some psychological studies have been made, says Cynthia Clark Wedel, suggesting women feel guilty because they can do their housekeeping and their cooking so easily. When instant coffee first came out, advertisers suggested how easy it was to pour a spoonful of coffee in a cup of hot water. Then the motivational research experts discovered that when women bought instant coffee they were sneaking in the grocery store and hiding the instant coffee at the bottom of their baskets. Why? Because women felt guilty about anything that was easy. They might like it, but they had no wish to admit it. Now instant coffee is not advertised as easy. It is delicious, good for the family, gracious.

Women spend endless time doing unnecessary things. They remember their mothers and grandmothers toiling endlessly at housework. Now that modern gadgets, TV dinners, frozen foods, prepared cake mixes, and so on, have made housework easy they feel a sense of uselessness and guilt. Their plight is made more difficult by the fact that while their roles are getting easier and easier, men are more and more under tension and pressure.

The sense of guilt that women feel because their work involves less drudgery than their mothers knew is altogether spurious. They have time, if they use it, for reading and for thinking, for cultural activities, and, best of all, more time for their children, more time to share themselves with their families. The ease of modern housekeeping is a blessing and a boon and there is no need for shame or guilt. There is no virtue in women doing unnecessary things just to make keeping house a burden.

Again, let it be noted, it is no sin to have leisure time. Why are we so uncomfortable if we are not doing something through every waking hour? Why is leisure a problem? In our modern culture we seem to pride ourselves on being tired, worn out, and weary. If we have time on our hands we feel guilty, as if energy had to be burned with endless abandon. No one will confess to not being busy, under strain.

Nevertheless, as automation transforms labor and provides

more and more leisure, and as housework becomes easier, we are inviting neuroses unless we learn to enjoy leisure and cultivate the art of contemplation. There is no guilt involved in quietly reading a book, taking a nap, watching a baseball game or playing golf. There is no sin attached to watching a sunset or bird watching. The privilege of leisure is the gift of modern culture to be received with gratitude. To be honest, I rejoice in times of leisure to do nothing at all.

ACCEPTANCE OF THE PAST

We do not need to complicate the problem of guilt, which is onerous enough, by fretting over issues without substance. We had best recognize the difference between sin and the problems thrust upon us by the patterns of contemporary society. It is sin that is our deepest problem, the guilty memories that haunt our days.

Basically, we have no choice but to accept the past and learn to live with our memories. We cannot alter yesterday. We can only find its wisdom for today. As Reilly observed in T. S. Eliot's *The Cocktail Party,*

> You will have to live with these memories and make them
> Into something new. Only by acceptance
> Of the past will you alter its meaning.[15]

It should be noted, however, that acceptance does not mean approval, nor does it mean surrender to the past. On the contrary, it means making memories "into something new" by using them as a means of wisdom for today.

Katherine Anthony notes, in *The Lambs,* that Charles and Mary Lamb destroyed themselves because they went on "endlessly expiating a guilt they never had accepted." Mary Lamb, who murdered her mother, and Charles, who condoned the act, spent their time in "determined forgetting," as if they could erase their sin from memory without coming to terms with it. As Katherine Anthony says,

Whenever the horror of the reality threatened to overwhelm them, Mary escaped into a mad sequence of dreams and Charles into a state of drunken unconsciousness. On awakening, they found the old spectre of conscience still there, but disguised as the face of bearable sins and omissions. Charles' drunkenness and Mary's insanity were within the realm of the mentionables—things that could be talked of in their letters. But the horror of matricide could not be borne with full consciousness.[16]

There was no escape for Charles and Mary Lamb in a process of "determined forgetting," which was beyond the realm of the possible, even in insanity and drunkenness.

Posterity never has wasted sympathy on poor, murdered Elizabeth Lamb. If Charles and Mary could have accepted their guilt, faced it relentlessly and atoned for it, they might have found their way through the years to come without destroying themselves. Unhappily, their evasions, their rationalizations, and their "determined forgetting" left them with nothing except their unacceptable memories and their unredeemed sin. They could not make their memories "into something new."

Charles and Mary Lamb provide a striking illustration, too, of the fact that the capacity to love and be loved is not primarily the consequence of rejection by others, but rather unacknowledged and unatoned personal guilt. Because they could not love themselves or accept themselves, they were decisively unlovable. Love presupposes a high level of personal integrity. I do not mean to say that love requires perfection, but rather the capacity to be honest, to avoid concealment. It is the anxiety of concealment that makes us both unlovable and incapable of love. We are isolated from God and man when we seek to hide the past without accepting it.

I cannot forget a woman who came to my office years ago, nervous, tense, with a worn and troubled look on her face. She told me she felt rejected, unloved, and unable to accept friendship even when it was proffered. "What's wrong with me?" she asked. Then, as if she knew the answer, she told the soiled and sordid story of her past. Tears flowed as she talked on and on. When she had finished, she remarked, "I feel better than I have felt for years."

In a moment of honest confession, the woman had accepted her past, acknowledged the consequences of it, and laid foundations for a new beginning with the anxiety of concealment laid to rest. One who had been nervous and tense, afraid of friendship, and desperately lonely, found her way to freedom and fellowship.

Seventy years ago one of the most important events in the world of psychology took place. As rarely happens in science, a man did something entirely new. He treated an intelligent young girl suffering from an hysterical disorder by simply listening to her for hundreds of hours. She talked herself out, finally, and Sigmund Freud had come by way of psychology to an ancient and unrelenting truth imbedded in the Christian faith, namely, that the confession and acceptance of the past mark the road to freedom and fellowship.

Without confession and acceptance of the past we learn nothing from the sins and follies of yesterday. We go on concealing, blaming others for the way we are, or trying to forget the unforgettable. Once we have confessed our sins and accepted the past and our responsibility for it, the road ahead is open with new possibilities and promise.

FORGIVENESS

To be sure, confession and acceptance are not enough. That is where psychology and the Christian faith so often divide. What we really need to make our memories "into something new" is forgiveness. It should be noted, however, that confession and acceptance of the past make forgiveness possible. There can be no forgiveness for unacknowledged sin, and surely no cleansing of the past for which we refuse to accept responsibility.

One of the paradoxes of life is the fact that environment shapes our attitudes and feelings and does much to determine whether or not we care for moral values. We know that slums breed crime and violence, but at the same time we hold delinquents from the slums responsible for their behavior. We may defend them on environmental grounds, point to the sordid conditions which fashioned their lives, and plead for a second chance for them. But there is no hope for their moral recovery unless they accept responsibility for themselves regardless of their environment.

We cannot forgive the misdemeanors of our children if they simply plead they did what they did because of the pressure of circumstances, or because they had to go along with the crowd. The redemption of the Prodigal Son began when he "came to himself." He accepted responsibility for his own stupidity and sin and said to himself, "I will arise and go to my father, and I will say to my father, 'Father, I have sinned.' " There would be no evasions, no excuses, no alibis. There would be, therefore, the possibility of forgiveness, and with it the promise of renewed fellowship.

The Prodigal, let it be noted, did not deserve forgiveness, and there are times when our children do not deserve to be forgiven. They misrepresent the truth and they do what they have been told not to do. They break our hearts and sometimes we feel the agony of pain. But we see their hurt, their regret, their inner turmoil, and we do forgive them because we love them. We put our arms around them and then we say, "You won't do it again, will you?" When they acknowledge their wrongness and accept responsibility for it we open the doors to comradeship and understanding.

Obviously, forgiveness cannot altogether mend what is past. There are inescapable consequences flowing from sin, whether it is acknowledged or not. There is a fine attached to speeding or running through a red light in the family car. There may be an accident with many lives involved. The sin of prejudice is costly, leaving social turmoil and conflict in its wake, and the sin of a cantankerous disposition may well play havoc with a family or a business office. Sin always has consequences, whether the sin is forgiven or not.

Forgiveness does not erase consequences. What it does is restore fellowship, relieve us of loneliness and isolation. The deepest pain sin occasions is not punishment, as such, but isolation. Watch a child with a guilty conscience, bearing in his mind a broken promise or some failure of obedience. We may not know what is troubling him, but we know he is not at ease in our presence. We cannot reach him, try as we will. We are excluded, shut away by the festering sin in his heart.

It is so in our experience with God. Something in us separates us from the love of God that will not let us go. We can endure punishment, but we cannot endure the sense of alienation from God. We cannot endure the self-broken bonds of love that isolate us in our own misery. We need to know that God "is faithful and just and will forgive our sins"[17] and restore us to fellowship. The wonder of it is that God does forgive, even when we do not deserve to be forgiven, for "God is love."

There is a suggestion of the nature of forgiveness in the experience of Arturo Toscanini who, at a rehearsal of the Metropolitan Opera in New York, swore at the orchestra in Italian and in his disgust said, also in Italian, that the orchestra "plays like pigs." When, subsequently, the Italian was translated the orchestra was offended and said it would not play for him until he apologized. To the mediator who came to see him, Toscanini explained that he could not apologize because the "orchestra plays like pigs." But he proposed the solution that worked: "I go to rehearsal and smile and say 'Good morning.' "

The orchestra, no doubt, did "play like pigs" on the occasion that troubled Toscanini. That was a fact that could not be altered. Evidently the orchestra was aware of its failure to perform adequately and found forgiveness and restoration in Toscanini's "Good morning," and in his radiant smile. The sin of the fumbled rehearsal remained sin, but the fellowship of the orchestra and its leader was restored. It should be added that out of the experience of reconciliation and forgiveness came great music and profound rapport between orchestra and leader.

GRATEFUL COMMITMENT

Under the impetus of Toscanini's forgiveness the orchestra, which had been working at cross purposes, expressed its gratitude in commitment. There was a change of mind in those who composed the orchestra which revived their capacity to create stirring music. In some such fashion we respond to the forgiveness of God with gratitude that overflows in the commitment of our lives to the highest. The ending of alienation by way of forgiveness is the priceless ingredient in moral recovery.

Consider a child forgiven for a misdemeanor. He cannot do

enough to compensate for the gratitude he feels. He will run errands, bring flowers from the garden to his mother, go to bed on time and without protest. To be sure, his gratitude may not last beyond nightfall, but while the glow of it remains he is "a new creation," his behavior almost beyond belief. The pain of his isolation was more than he could endure and his gratitude for renewed fellowship was a pearl of great price.

What God yearns to do is to restore us to fellowship, to reconcile us to Himself, as Paul said, and to save us from lonely isolation in the prison of our own sin. That is the glory of the gospel which inspires endless gratitude. Not deserving forgiveness, not able to earn it, we are accepted by the love of God. We sing the truth in a well-loved hymn:

> Not the labors of my hands,
> Can fulfil Thy laws' demands.
>
> . . . .
>
> Naked come to Thee for dress,
> Helpless look to Thee for grace.[18]

Bankrupt morality is made solvent by grace and in freedom we sing psalms of thanksgiving.

What is more, in our thanksgiving we make music with our lives. Our own little flutes or violins are caught up in the grandeur of eternal music, and our thin little stream of sound is magnified and enriched by the fellowship of many notes that harmonize and sing. We are not alone. On the contrary, we are one with the community of the faithful.

I'm Sorry for Me

A SMALL GIRL, weeping ruefully over a broken doll, spoke for multitudes when she said, "I'm sorry for me." She spoke for a discouraged man who did not receive a promotion he had toiled to win, and for a young man who missed a college scholarship by a fraction of a point. She spoke for a young woman whose fiancé married her best friend, and for a young lady who left college because she missed being pledged to the sorority of her choice.

All of these and multitudes of others have one thing in common: they are isolated in their own self-pity, imprisoned by their brooding preoccupation with their own misery. The doors of communication are tightly shut and their capacity to share the lives of others is attenuated. They can think of nothing but their own frustration and inner distaste for life that seems to leave them with empty hands and bruised hearts.

The portrait of Elijah is an unforgettable one because it finds us where we are. The ancient prophet was a lonely man and he was frightened by the fury of Jezebel, who threatened his life. He had opposed the queen and bested her pagan priests. Then, exhausted and frightened, he took to his heels. After a day's journey into the wilderness he "sat down under a broom tree," wishing he could die on the spot. He fell asleep.

When Elijah awakened, he took off again and climbed Mount Horeb. There, he thought, he would be safe from the vengeance of Jezebel. He found a cave, slipped through its yawning opening, and there confronted the turmoil of his own mind. With vivid Oriental imagery he described his experience. A "strong wind rent the mountains, and broke in pieces the rocks," and "after the wind an earthquake" shook the foundations of the earth, and "after the earthquake a fire."

Of course, the wind, the earthquake, and the fire were not outside, but inside the mind of Elijah. He was shaken by fear, mingled with shame, and he burned with regret and inner turbulence. The foundations of his life and his faith were shaken. Life seemed too much for him and the struggle beyond his strength. Absorbed in self-pity, Elijah was ready to quit.

The experience of Elijah is a reasonable facsimile of the experience of many of us. Our lives are not threatened and we do not run away to the wilderness, but our emotional reactions to struggle and frustration are akin to his. We blunder into moods of depression and near despair trying to cope with our days. Now and then we feel as Elijah felt when he said, "It is enough; now, O Lord, take away my life."

Every little while some discouraged man or woman says to me, "I wish I could die." Disappointments come and we are shaken as Elijah was shaken by earthquake, wind, and fire on Mount Horeb. We find ourselves in conflict, and under the strain of it we feel overwhelmed and alone. We lend our strength to worthy causes and then meet animosity and opposition until we wonder why we should go on. We wish we could find a refuge somewhere and let the world ruin itself in its own way.

SELF-PITY

Self-pity comes upon us in various guises. Frequently we are disposed to feel we are asked to carry loads that are, as we say, "Just too much." A disturbed man was quite certain that at the office he was expected to do more than his rightful share of the work. When others left at five o'clock, he watched them go resentfully and then remained to toil late into the evening. Several hours of counseling revealed the fact he did not need to remain at the office overtime. On the contrary, he rather enjoyed his own self-pity. It was his way of affirming a self-importance he did not really feel.

Often, even in adulthood, we are like a four-year-old boy who fell part way down the stairs. He was not really hurt, but the tears flowed copiously and his mother held him in her arms.

After a few moments she said, "Now you are all right." To which he responded, "O.K. Now I go fall down again." The attentions of his mother more than compensated for his bruises and he hoped that when he fell again his mother would once again feel sorry for him. So he could affirm his own significance.

We are quite sure, at times, nobody else has problems as difficult as ours or burdens as heavy. We feel alone and sorry for ourselves, and yet we would be lost if the loads we think we must carry did not inspire the sympathy of others. There is no sorrow like our sorrow and no pain like our pain. We think we have been set apart to suffer and to struggle more than most of humankind.

One troubled woman remarked, "My husband travels and is away nine months out of twelve. I'm left at home with the children, the house and the housework, and it is more than I can endure." I could understand her feeling, her loneliness, and the weight of her task. But she seemed to feel that her problem was unique, as if she alone had a traveling husband. Somehow she had come to believe that the fates had conspired to make life difficult for her. She wished she could die if it were not for the children.

Under the strain of life it is easy for all of us to become obsessed by our own problems. Vardis Fisher says of Thomas Wolfe, the novelist, that "Wolfe obsessed Wolfe. Self-pity was the disease in him."[1] There is, of course, self-pity in all of us, but "in Wolfe it was a tyrant," a demon, if you please. Nobody's troubles were quite like Wolfe's troubles.

To be sure, there may be times when our troubles are a strain and we feel momentarily "put upon." At such times self-pity can easily become the disease of the moment. And yet, when we are honest with ourselves we know we only share the common lot of multitudes. The isolation we impose upon ourselves because we think we must bear too much is self-imposed.

SEEING STRAIGHT

It should be noted, too, that under the stress of strain things often get out of perspective. The problems we ought to meet in stride assume undue proportions; molehills turn into mountains that cannot be moved. We see things not as they are, but jaundiced by our own feelings. Our emotions play tricks on us and play havoc with our reason and our common sense.

Curiously, when feelings of self-pity disturb our inner world, the world around us appears antagonistic. There is a suggestion of what happens in the discovery that the personalities of chickens can be altered by fitting them with contact lenses. Al Schriner, a Santa Rosa, California, poultry man, makes contact lenses for chickens and turns out one hundred and fifty thousand pairs of tiny eyepieces for barnyard fowl every day. The lenses, made of molded plastic, fit snugly over the eyeball.

Unlike human contact lenses, which help people to see better, the lenses for chickens have built-in distortion which causes them to see less accurately. The reason is simple. "Modern methods of raising chickens cause severe social problems among them, not unlike those experienced by humans in crowded areas of big cities," says Al Schriner. "Chickens on big poultry farms no longer run in fields where they have to scratch and pick for a living, but are confined in cages or crowded houses where food and water are handy."[2]

Inevitably, the chickens have more time to scratch and pick at each other. With the lenses, the chickens can see well enough to eat and drink, but not well enough to fight with their neighbors. They become more tranquil and less excitable and less inclined to pick, jump, and fly about. Their distorted vision makes them complacent and indifferent to their surroundings.

In somewhat the same fashion our inner distortions of external reality make us unwilling to risk struggle. We find alibis for inertia and retreat. We tell ourselves the odds against us are too great. We magnify our difficulties and minimize our spiritual resources. We overemphasize our problems and deemphasize the powers that are ours to cope with them. What we see is not reality, but illusion. Carl Jung, the psychologist, put the truth wisely when he wrote, "How can anyone see straight when he does not even see himself and that darkness which he himself carries unconsciously into all his dealings?"[3]

The inner darkness of self-pity leaves us with distorted vision of the world around us and of our relation to it. It seems to us that others have the best of things and that we always come off second best. So it is that we are alienated from our fellows with a resentment that leaves us self-imprisoned and alone.

GREETING THE DAY

There are times, too, when we simply get out of the wrong side of the bed, feeling glum and out-of-sorts. The lines of Samuel Smith's lovely hymn seem curiously deceptive:

> The morning light is breaking,
> The darkness disappears.[4]

The morning light has dawned outside, but inside the darkness remains. We are unable to command the morning with creative zest because our minds are vagrants.

Today's possibilities are destroyed by the memory of yesterday's disappointments and failures. The irritations of yesterday crowd into the mind at dawning like a horde of angry mosquitoes intent on destroying our poise. Yesterday's hurts, festering through a sleepless night, pour their poison into the morning to leave unholy marks on the newness of the day. Yesterday's disappointments hang like heavy clouds over the dawn, shutting out the light. We do not command the morning; the morning is commanded by the regrets of yesterday. Instead of saying, "Good morning, God," we are disposed to say, "Good God, it's morning."

Or, quite possibly, today becomes a thing of shreds and patches because tomorrow looms forbiddingly beyond. There are fears that focus in tomorrow and they thwart the promise of today. Anxieties crowd the mind, reaching out like the tentacles of an octopus, from the unfathomed future. There is nothing wrong with the morning. It dawns as it always does. "The morning steals upon the night, melting the darkness," and there is the glory of the sunrise, if we get up in time to see it. There is dew or frost on the grass as usual, and the trees lift their graceful limbs to the sky as is their customary habit. The trouble comes from our minds. It comes from the invasion of yesterday and tomorrow. The past and the future are aggressors against the peace and the promise of today.

It is curious the way our minds ramble hither and yon, collecting disagreeable thoughts unless we take command with positive affirmations and great thoughts. We look out the window at the cold, drizzling weather, and we say to ourselves: "This is a miserable, disgusting day," and our spirits fall until they reflect the weather.

It is fatal to begin the morning with the spirit of Edna St. Vincent Millay who noted disconsolately, "Life must go on. I forget just why." Days are full of disaster and despair when we greet the morning in the mood of A. E. Housman:

> Yonder see the morning blink:
> The sun is up, and up must I,
> To wash and dress and eat and drink
> And look at things and talk and think
> And work, and God knows why.[5]

You and God had better know why!

I would literally hate to get up in the morning if I had no sense of meaning or mission for the day. I would hate to get up just to get and spend. I think, as the old song says, "I'd like to murder the bugler" sounding reveille if I had to get up to plod through another meaningless day. Life would be utterly futile and the dawn full of distaste if I felt like Thomas Hardy's Tess, who complained that the stars are like apples, some good, some blighted. "We live on a blighted one," she says sadly.

But our star is not blighted. It is full of wonders to be understood, love to be experienced, truth to be found, goodness and beauty to be appreciated. Have you never felt like Jacob wrestling through the hours with an angel and saying: "I will not let you go until you bless me"?[6] There are new insights to be won in the struggle of today, new depths of character to be sounded, new knowledge of God to be won. At the dawn of every day there is a summons, "Something waiting, go and find it."

Ernie Pyle sensed the meaning of days infused with purposes and objectives while he lived at the front in the days of the Second World War. He noted what he called "the magnificent

simplicity" of life at the front. It was life consisting only of the
essentials—food, sleep, transportation, and "what little warmth
and safety a man could manage to wangle out of it by personal
ingenuity." Normally, I suppose, a life stripped to bare neces-
sities would be boring. But time passed rapidly. Says Pyle, "A
whole month would be gone before I knew it."

What gave life at the front its meaning was a sense of objectives to be won, a feeling of comradeship in a meaningful cause.
Life was being given to something, spent for purposes loosely
defined as "the four freedoms." There was, says Ernie Pyle, "a
feeling of vitality, of being in the heart of everything, of being a
part of it—no mere onlooker, but a member of the team."

How we feel about the days, whether we have a "feeling of
vitality," or a haunting self-pity hinges on the mental stance with
which we greet the day. Inevitably we are sorry for ourselves and
alienated from the goodness of life if we got out of the wrong side
of the bed.

THE DAILY ROUND

There is, then, a fourth guise under which self-pity falls on us.
It is the assumption that the routine is the unusual and the
unique. We often overlook the simple fact that much of life is a
matter of plodding through desert places to reach some temporary oasis, after which the plodding begins again. We forget that
every achievement is nine-tenths drudgery and struggle, and
burdens that seem too heavy are more normal than otherwise.

Winston Churchill spent most of his life plodding. Nobody
thought he was a genius, not by any stretch of the imagination. He
rated as a hack writer or a second-rate politician, and those
around him often conspired to make his intellectual and political
journeyings as unpleasant as possible.

Most youngsters seem to think that the grind of going to school
is mostly a matter of doing what they would rather not. That is
especially true in the spring. School gets to be a dull routine, the
same old road to the same old place every morning. Day after day
there are the same teachers in the same rooms pouring on the
inevitable assignments. If there is any Jerusalem in the distance,

it seems too far removed to make much difference. Madye Lee Chastain summarized the feelings of a striking collection of youngsters in her story, "Fripsey Fun." When the youngsters were home for Christmas one of them remarked, "It's the best dull year we've had yet."

I dare say most of us spend more time in struggle than we ever are likely to spend in triumph. Life is mostly one routine job after another. Orlo Choguill comments pertinently that the most dismal thing about milking cows is that the cows never stay milked. And, I suspect, the most dismal thing about most of life is that cows never stay milked; dishes never stay washed; beds never stay made; and the house never stays cleaned. No matter how you look at it, there always is the "daily round, the common task" that never stays done.

The trouble in business, too, is that "the cows never stay milked." You get your desk cleared of the correspondence, but it will not stay that way. You satisfy a customer today, but tomorrow you have to get him satisfied all over again. You get your organization running smoothly, and the moment you turn your back things are at sixes and sevens. You have an uneasy feeling that you are in struggle most of the time. Sometimes I feel that way. Every time I finish preaching one sermon, I have to start another.

No matter who we are, we have to grapple with a lot of dullness, and sweat through the disagreeable along the road where we are going. Of course, nobody outside sees the dullness, the wearisome routine. That is why it is so dull and so lonely. Nobody understood the drudgery of twenty years of struggle that lay behind Thackeray's *Vanity Fair*. Everybody saw the finished product and acclaimed it, but nobody knew the years of struggle that lay behind the triumph.

There were times, I am sure, when Thackeray said in one way or another, "I'm sorry for me," and yet his was a routine passage, akin to that of all who win at least a measure of triumph in our common life. There is no easy, rutless road from where we are to where we hope to go. Pain and sorrow, frustration and defeat come alike to all and there is nothing unusual about trouble and hardship except that they are usual. Even when things are running smoothly for us there is likely to be trouble around the corner. As Browning once wrote to a friend, "When we are safest there's a sunset touch, and that's the time when the applecart is apt to go over—when we're safest, or think we are."

THE PERSONAL EQUATION

The problem of life, therefore, is to handle upsets when and where they come without floundering into self-pity. The dictionary suggests by way of synonyms that to be upset is to be "overturned, disordered, capsized," or simply to be "mentally disturbed." There is a difference, however, between being "capsized" by self-pity and being "mentally disturbed." It is one thing to be sunk and it is something else to be troubled. The problem is to work our way through troubles and difficulties without being capsized and sunk. The apostle Paul expressed the idea admirably when he wrote, concerning the early Christians, "We are afflicted in every way, but not crushed; perplexed, but not driven to despair."[7]

St. Paul recognized the often unobserved fact that every problem has in it a personal equation. On one hand we have a concrete situation that in itself is upsetting. But on the other hand, we have ourselves as the instruments with which to meet the circumstances. The situation may very well have in it all the ingredients necessary to destroy equilibrium, and still we succeed in meeting it with assurance, deftness, and poise. A week later, however, a comparable situation leaves us in a state of collapse.

Frequently a problem that gets the best of us on Monday turns out to be no problem at all on Wednesday, or vice versa. On Wednesday when Johnny spilled his orange juice after being late for breakfast, we met the situation with cheerful grace and sent Johnny off to school on an even keel. All day, thereafter, we felt a warm glow of satisfaction. But on Monday, three days before, when Johnny came to breakfast wearing the wrong clothes and feeling in an argumentative mood, we exploded. Thereafter, the whole day went wrong.

The situations were comparable, but the personal equations were altogether different. So it is all through life. One day we meet frustration with faith and courage and a week later we meet disappointment and we collapse in despair. Today we seize trouble by the throat and conquer it, and tomorrow we fall apart at the seams. Last month we had a staggering problem to meet and we met it with assurance and competence. A month later a minor problem overwhelmed us.

The inescapable conclusion is that what upsetting situations do to us depends on what they find in us. Despite the hounding circumstances that made life difficult for the Psalmist and inspired his cry: "Be gracious to me, O Lord, for I am in distress,"[8] he came through on an even keel. Observe how he concludes the recital of his troubles. "Love the Lord, all you his saints. The Lord preserves the faithful . . . Be strong, and let your heart take courage, all you who wait for the Lord."[9]

TAKING DISAPPOINTMENT IN STRIDE

Upsetting situations are disastrous, however, if they find resentment in us. Notice, if you will, that there was no resentment in the Psalmist. He was not mad at anybody. He was "in distress," facing an upsetting situation, but he was grateful for the strength and courage he had found to keep him on his feet. The personal factor was decisive. It always is. We can meet problem situations and discouragements with resentful self-pity or with gratitude for strength to deal with them.

I recall a high-school student, a star diver on the swimming team. He injured his back and was told he would have to wear a cast for six months. When he came home with his body encased in plaster of Paris he said to his mother, "Mother, I don't want you to feel sorry for me." She replied, "Oh, I'm not sorry for you. I was just wondering how the girls can autograph your cast." He smiled and wore his cast until his back was supposedly healed.

As the years went on, he went on diving, but always troubled by his back. In college, in the middle of a winning season the doctors ordered the young man to give up diving permanently or suffer irreparable injury to his back. He took the disappointment in his stride, taught himself to play a banjo and a guitar, organized a combo, and with the group went on two summer cruise ships as an entertainer.

Neither resentment nor self-pity intruded into the young man's life to spoil it. If he could not dive, he could express himself in some other way. So can we all if we avoid resentment that disorders the mind and stirs the emotions. If one road is blocked another always is open if we do not clutter the highway with landslides of self-pity and bitterness.

Resentment is an invitation to self-pity and loneliness because it builds barriers in us which thwart comfortable fellowship and make it impossible for us to find compensations beyond the barriers to our hopes. As one resentful woman remarked, "I feel at odds with God and with everyone else."

ESCAPE VS. DISCIPLINE AND PERSEVERANCE

We often wish for some easy way around or through the difficulties that leave us depressed and sorry for ourselves. And yet it is only as we begin to deal with ourselves and to accept the fact that the "fault is not in our stars," but "in ourselves" that we are able to move out of imprisonment and misery and into the light of day. Indeed, it is in the relentless discipline of ourselves that life finds new meaning and value.

Back in 1932 a book appeared in Warsaw by a Pole, Stanislaw Ignacy Witkiewicz, which suggests we may approach our difficulties from another direction. The Pole was something of a philosopher as well as a sensitive observer of the current scene, and he called his novel *Insatiability*. He pictured the decay of the world as he experienced it in the forties and fifties. His heroes were unhappy, without faith, and with no sense of meaning in anything they did. The atmosphere of decay and dismal senselessness extended throughout the world he pictured.

While the world was falling into decay and men were seeing themselves as nothing, a vast number of hawkers and super-salesmen appeared in the cities peddling "Murti-Bing" pills. Murti-Bing was a Mongolian philosopher who had succeeded in producing an organic means of injecting a philosophy of life painlessly. The "philosophy of life" was contained in Murti-Bing pills in an extremely condensed form. A man who used the pills became serene and happy. His problems became superficial and unimportant. He smiled indulgently at those who continued to worry about them. What is more, Murti-Bing pills completely eliminated man's spiritual hunger. He could endure anything with unquestioning complacency.

The trouble with Murti-Bing pills was that while they relieved man of his tensions, his troubles, his fears, and gave him serenity, they also left him totally devoid of the will to reach any Promised Land. They were a psychological and spiritual anesthetic and nothing more. They simply enabled those who used them to submit to their condition without distress or protest. So, users of the pills were easily conquered and subdued by a vigorous enemy intent on world domination.

Wise men would avoid Murti-Bing pills like the plague. There is no salvation for us in escape from irritations and problems. On the contrary, salvation lies in accepting the challenge of the hardships and hurts we are tempted to resent and to seek spiritual resources for dealing with them. It is one thing to say, "I can't, so I will adjust with Murti-Bing pills," but it is something else to say, "I can and I will carry on with courage in the power of God."

The upshot of the matter is that the creative possibilities of a disturbing situation await the spiritual "pause that refreshes" our minds. "Be gracious to me, O Lord, for I am in distress"[10] is as good a beginning as any. At least the Psalmist paused long enough to bring God into his problem. He did not just strike out on his own, blindly and bitterly. He waited in quietness for wisdom and strength and then moved creatively into the situation, avoiding the misery of self-pity.

Half of our blundering futility and self-pity come from our unwillingness to stop and to think. It was Albert Schweitzer who noted that we push ahead blindly because we are suffering from the "intoxication of activity." We react to situations without thinking or praying; we do not respond creatively to trouble in what the gospels call "the power of the spirit." There is a glorious word from a wise man that was written for our condition: "For still the vision awaits its time . . . If it seems slow, wait for it; it will surely come, it will not delay."[11]

When I was a boy, impetuous as boys are, my father used to quote a poem, all of which I have forgotten except the first line:

"Before you decide, think it through!" As he saw it, upsetting situations are a spiritual challenge. There is a suggestion of what I mean in Howard Taubman's description of Toscanini preparing an orchestra for a concert. For Toscanini, the only person who mattered at a concert or in an opera house was the composer; the only thing that concerned him was the musical intention of the composer, and to get to the secret of that he would spare neither himself nor anyone else. If he got irritated, and he sometimes did, it was not because he could not get this or that "effect," but because it hurt him as much to hear a masterpiece being made to say the wrong thing, or the right thing in the wrong tone of voice, as it would to see a noble statue mutilated or a great painting cut to ribbons.

Toscanini's upsets were not occasions for self-pity. On the contrary, they were a challenge to achieve the high expectations of the composer. So our irritations and unwanted burdens are a challenge to meet the high expectations of God for us. In the face of our troubles we can say the right thing in the right tone of voice if we pause long enough to feel the challenge. We can meet threat of Communism with great positive devotion to the best in our heritage if we see our peril as a spiritual challenge. We do not need to say the wrong thing with repression and coercion if we can understand that the present hour of upset is a stirring opportunity to fulfill the expectations of the Composer of our lives and our freedom.

In the days when England was beset by war and half destroyed by bombing, A. E. Housman wrote soberly: "These were days when Heaven was falling, the hour when earth's foundations fled." Then he spoke of "the casual youngsters of the Royal Air Force," who calmly accepted the challenge of their times and "whose shoulders held the sky suspended."[12] The phrase is a striking one. And, quite possibly our shoulders can hold the sky suspended when the situation around us is perilous. It is not a dead-end street to be resented or feared, it is a challenge to be met with the power of God and the wisdom of God.

Again, if we are willing to wait, to experience the spiritual pause that refreshes, we will see burdensome situations as invitations to spiritual growth and not as occasions for self-pity. Nevil

Shute summarizes the matter in his novel *Pastoral,* wherein a middle-aged Dane finds himself in an office, upset by a Mr. Marshall, owner of the business. The Dane took a great deal of unjust abuse from his boss, but his Lutheran heritage had taken deep root, and when a friend suggested he might as well quit, he replied: "I think it is not the right time to go. When things are not good, then one should stay and help to get them right again."[13]

Exactly so, for it is in the staying that we grow, in setting things right when they are wrong. A small boy inadvertently came to grips with a vital truth when he was leading his sister up a mountain path. She complained, "It's not a path at all. It's all rocky and bumpy." "Sure," he answered, "the bumps are what you climb on." If we have learned anything from our experience of life it is that we climb on the bumps, and when the bumps are most irksome it is precisely the time to keep climbing and growing.

It is surprising to discover how many great things have come out of great difficulties men or women used as steppingstones to spiritual power. When Handel was facing heartbreak and disappointment, he turned to the Scriptures and read from Isaiah, "He was despised and rejected of men." The words seem to have been written for him and he says his "whole being glowed with creative passion." The result was Handel's "Messiah." John Milton, upset by the tragedy of his own blindness, translated his loss into the insight and beauty of *Paradise Lost.* Goethe's mother used to say that whenever her son was haunted by grief, he always turned the burden into a poem and so came through.

HOPE BEYOND REBUFF

It is suggestive to notice that the journeying Jews making a pilgrimage to Jerusalem from afar often found themselves on rugged, waterless roads that tried their souls. The Psalmist wrote, however, that "As they go through the valley of Baca [weeping] they make it a place of springs."[14] They recognized that "the valley of weeping" was only an episode on the road to their destination. They could endure hardship and even pain for the sake of Jerusalem. What carried them through the hard places was their vision of the Holy City beyond. They turned the grim valley into a place of spiritual springs because they were looking ahead.

No man can

> . . . welcome each rebuff
> That turns earth's smoothness rough,[15]

without some hope beyond rebuff. But burdensome days can be met and gotten over if we do not lose sight of tomorrow. Edward Gibbon, the great historian, tells us that he spent twenty years in the "valley of weeping," working year after year on his book *The Decline and Fall of the Roman Empire.* Two things saved him from being sorry for himself. One was the dream that some day he would finish his work and give the world the fruit of his labor. The other was the fact that he looked forward to every day as an opportunity to learn something about the Romans that neither he nor anyone else had discovered before. Quite literally, he could not wait for tomorrow in anticipation of what tomorrow might teach him. It was so with Noah Webster, toiling for thirty-five years in the discouraging valley while he wrote his dictionary. Can you imagine anything more drab and disheartening than compiling a dictionary? And yet, Noah Webster notes that his sense of wonder never left him. What would tomorrow bring? What new word or shade of meaning would he uncover?

No matter how dark and discouraging the valley may be, we dare not lose our sense of "something evermore to be." The writer of the inspiring book of Hebrews caught the truth in a glorious phrase when he wrote that Jesus, "for the joy that was set before him"[16] kept His feet on the ground and endured a crown of thorns and a cross. In passing "through the valley of Baca [weeping]" He made it "a place of springs."[17]

TRUST IN GOD

Sometimes I wonder why God did not make the world without any "valleys of weeping" in it. Why do we have to face suffering and disappointment, failure and distress? Now and then I get into

Job's mood when I see men and women struggling through the dark valley. I come up with Job's question: "Why is light given to a man whose way is hid, whom God has hedged in?"[18] Why are good men "hedged in" by the forbidding walls of dark valleys? Why do men and women who seem to be "the salt of the earth" find themselves disappointed and hurt, burdened by sorrow and disappointment? Only the other evening after a call I came home with those questions turning over and over in my mind. I knew all the stock answers. Job's three friends covered them all a good many centuries ago. In the end, like Job, I came up with the mystery of God. I came face to face with the mystery of a triumphant Cross!

As for Job, you will remember that he was not a patient man. He was angry in his "valley of weeping," full of self-pity, and he wanted to know why he was there. He did not deserve it, did he? He hurled that question into the heavens, and God let him complain and struggle with logic. Then God spoke "in the whirlwind,"

> Where were you when I laid the foundation of the earth?
> . . . .
> Who laid its cornerstone,
> When the morning stars sang together?[19]

Were you there, Job? Maybe you will learn some day that I am God, and I know what I am about. "Your ways are not my ways and my ways are not your ways." My love will not fail you, Job, but you must trust me through light and dark, through valleys and shadows. Then Job said out of the depths of his suffering: "Though he slay me, yet will I trust him."[20]

I do not know why the "valley of weeping" is one of life's inevitables, but I do know that by trusting God we can make it "a place of springs." We can travel gratefully through discouragement and hurt if we will trust God to lead us through the valley and out of it wiser and better than we were. David Grayson caught an echo of the truth when he described a passenger he met once on an ocean voyage. The man had good books on his cabin shelf, and on his stand the picture of a boy, his only son. One night he read to Grayson a poem he had written for his son. He had composed it, he said, "in the nights when I find it hard to sleep." The refrain, repeated at the end of each verse, bound up in few words what the man had learned on the voyage of his life. "Plow on, my son, plow on." Plow on, my son, plow on. Plow on through "the valley of weeping," plow on in trust, and make it "a place of springs." Plow on through toil and tears to the springs of life in God.

We will come, in the end, to the mystery of the triumphant Cross of Jesus Christ. See the picture, if you will. The clouds were dark over Calvary and a howling mob blocked the Via Dolorosa. Caesar's soldiers pressed their mounts against the surging mob to clear the way. Alone on the road was a tired man, his face streaked with blood from the thorns that pressed upon his head. He carried a heavy wooden cross whose weight was more than human strength could carry far. Stumbling, he fell into the dust of the road and the mob roared with derision and laughter. Some spit upon him to show their contempt. What an hour of defeat and agony in "the valley of weeping," and yet what an hour of redeeming power! The wooden cross that bent the Master to the earth and later held His broken body became the symbol of eternal springs. His "valley of weeping" is our "place of springs." His trust in God made His darkest valley into a "place of springs" for all Christendom through all the ages.

Why did it have to be? Why must we follow Him bearing crosses through our valleys? I do not know, but in retrospect I am grateful for the challenge of the lonely valley and for the promise that flowing springs are the everlasting answer to our trust while we are in it.

8

Isolated by Illness

Illness is one of life's inevitabilities. Sooner or later we are laid on the shelf at least temporarily when the machinery of the body goes askew. Rarely does anybody go through life without a bout or two with illness and suffering somewhere along the road. We become victims of germs or ailments of one sort or another. Some people are in ill health most of the time. They are in and out of hospitals and never enjoy robust health. They would give a great deal to be really well year in and year out.

On three or four occasions I have been relegated to hospitals, and for more than thirty years I have been visiting patients put on the shelf because of illness. I remember nothing about my first experience in a hospital. Like most youngsters of my generation, I had my tonsils removed. No doubt my parents painted the operation in its most pleasant colors before the event, just as my wife and I did when our sons were preparing to undergo the same experience. Everything went swimmingly when our second son prepared for the ordeal. We got him into a hospital gown with much laughing and good humor. He climbed onto the stretcher on wheels and an intern began pushing him down the hall toward the operating room. Suddenly he sat bolt upright and said, "I think I'd like to go home now."

That, I suspect, is very much the way we all feel before pending operations. We muster our courage for what is necessary, but we have misgivings about putting our bodies at the disposal of even the finest surgeons. We wonder if we might get by without the ordeal. How we would like to go home!

The first hospital experience I remember vividly came when I was a graduate student at Boston University. I had arrived in Boston with just enough money to pay my tuition and had thirty dollars left. So, with a sense of urgency I found two part-time jobs to pay my way while I studied. Too much work and too little sleep took their toll and shortly after Christmas I became sick. My roommate did his best to care for me, but I got worse and worse. A doctor whose name we found in the telephone book turned out to have been a quack. With my temperature soaring to 104°, my roommate finally bundled me into a taxicab and deposited me in the emergency room of the Massachusetts General Hospital.

By that time I had a five-day beard, and since the glands of my neck were badly swollen, the doctor had prescribed a black substance which I had dutifully smeared on my neck. My appearance belied the fact I was a reasonably respectable citizen and, I learned later, I was taken to a ward usually reserved for the least desirable patients. There were ten of us in the ward. One middle-aged man was having delirium tremens at the moment I was rolled into the ward and onto the bed I would occupy for the next three weeks.

Nobody paid any attention to me until the following morning. I was too ill to care. A nurse cleaned me up and washed the black from my neck. Then began a procession of interns who pricked my fingers repeatedly, taking samples of my blood. They asked innumerable questions, took my blood pressure, listened to my chest and told me nothing. I was just a name on a chart, a guinea pig for experimenting doctors. While my temperature remained high, my psychological temperature was as low as it could get.

I shared the feeling of Leonard Kriegel who as a youngster was paralyzed by polio. In describing his hospital experience he wrote: "I took an instant dislike to the doctor. Somehow I felt that he saw in me a body, an object for his probing science. Never did I feel that I was a fellow human being for him, or, for that matter, for any of the other doctors there. I would lie in my bed, listening to his clipped voice as he dictated his reports to Mrs. Ralston, furious, because I felt that for him I wasn't even there. There were times when he would stand at the side of the bed, so apparently oblivious to my presence as he talked or fiddled with my chart that it wouldn't have surprised me to have him look up and say, 'I'm sorry. I forgot you were still alive.' "[1]

How I wanted to go home! Unfortunately, home was two thousand miles away. The nights were horrible. I never knew men could snore in so many keys or with such personal flourishes. I buried my head under the pillow, but I still could hear the chorus. One man on the other side of the ward died and when the bed had been changed, in came a replacement suffering from lead poisoning. He screamed with pain most of the night. I felt trapped and helpless, lost and alone.

A doctor finally told me I had a bad case of pneumonia and that I would have to remain where I was until my lungs had entirely cleared. A barber came one day and removed my beard. I felt better, but I could not get used to being absolutely nobody in a collection of other nobodies. I was a patient, completely "other-directed." I did what I was told to do when I was told to do it. Everything was impersonal.

By the end of the first week I felt like sitting up in bed once or twice a day, but I was getting worried. Classes at the university continued to meet while I was absent and falling behind. Would my jobs be waiting for me when I got out of the hospital? My roommate at the university assured me that when I felt able to study he would bring my books and the assignments. He also went to the places where I worked and then told me not to worry about my jobs. Nevertheless, I worried just the same.

There was plenty of time for thinking, but most of my thinking was not exactly creative. My loneliness was overwhelming and I was very sorry for myself. Would I be able to carry on when I got out of the hospital? Would I be so far behind with my studies that I could not make the grade? Why did this have to happen to me? My plans and hopes were tumbling down around my ears and my mood was "black as the pit from pole to pole." My anxieties, fears, and depression did not speed my recovery.

When I finally emerged from the hospital, more than a little unsteady on my legs, I went back to my jobs and my studies and managed to finish and be graduated on schedule. Since that time

I often have thought of my own feelings of loneliness and despair, frustration and helplessness as I have visited with patients suffering from a variety of ills. In single rooms or in wards, wealthy or poor, they share the feelings I felt so many years ago.

THE SHOCK OF ILLNESS

When we are well we take our good health for granted, as if we deserved our good fortune. We are endowed with a body which is "self-nourishing, self-regulating, self-repairing, self-starting, and self-reproducing, lasting, like a good grandfather clock, for three quarters of a century." It is provided, as Lin Yu-tang notes, "with wireless vision and wireless hearing. It has a system for filing reports and impressions through a vast complex of nerves. It goes about with perfect knee action, and its amazing motor is completely silent."[2] If anything gets out of kilter, the mechanism usually fixes itself in time. God created the human body that way. It seems curious that, when we are in good health, we congratulate ourselves.

Illness is a rude shock to the ego. David Grayson describes his experience in a hospital during his first serious illness. Until he got to the hospital he was somebody. He gave instructions, managed his own affairs, and was reasonably independent. But in the hospital he was only a chart with a number on it. Nurses fed and bathed him and told him what he could and what he could not do. When he asked the doctors for information he got nothing but evasions. He was ordered to eat what he did not like and not to eat what he did like. His life was completely managed by a collection of men and women in white. He was an object, not a subject. Grayson was annoyed and deflated. He described his experience by saying:

Illness, like its elder brother, death, is a cessation. Life stops. Identity blurs. One hangs up his personality with his clothes in the closet and becomes a case—the patient in No. 12. No longer quite a man, but a condition, a problem, stretched out there for daily examination, looked down upon, peered into, charted on paper with graphs like the rise and fall in the price of wheat. It is this indignity even more than the pain and the weakness and the boredom that makes the experience, for a man with any imagination, difficult to bear. To be something, and then to be nothing! It is no doubt one of the commonest of human experiences—since I myself have known it, it seems as though all the world had been ill—and yet no one can ever know, for himself, until it has come to him, what it means to be set aside, lifted arrogantly out of his active labour, and put down horizontal and helpless in bed.[3]

I have no doubt that St. Paul suffered a serious blow to his ego when he found himself quite helpless in the hands of Luke, his physician. There is some evidence suggesting Paul tried to manage his own case and tell both Luke and God to get him on his feet quickly. Unhappily, he had to give up and let Luke manage things for a while, no matter how distasteful it might be. Paul could not cure himself and he knew it. What is more, no matter how urgently he mustered his will power he could not get up and go on with business as usual. He was whipped by his "thorn in the flesh."

When we are stopped by a germ so tiny we cannot see it or by some ailment that puts us to bed, we suffer a blow to pride. Conversely, however, a shock to the ego is likely to focus attention on the self. We get to thinking about ourselves or worrying about ourselves. It hurts our pride, too, when we discover that the world manages to get along reasonably well without us.

Everything about illness conspires to keep us humble. After a while it seems, as Peter Bowman notes, as if

> The stars that had pinned up the curtain of darkness
> Are beginning to loosen and fall spinning into the sea,[4]

so we flounder into overweening self-concern. As one woman said to another after visiting a mutual friend, "If she could get her mind off herself she would be all right."

BEING A PATIENT

When we head for the hospital for repairs of one sort or another it is important at the outset to accept the simple fact that for a while somebody is going to take over the management of our lives and our affairs. It won't do any good to protest, and resistance is altogether futile. Breakfast will come on schedule and the dietician and the doctor will determine whether it is to be ham and eggs or dry toast and tea. We do not give orders; we are told when to lie down and when to sit up. Nobody jumps when we say frog. In the hospital we are in the hands of men and women who are there to manage us. We had better get used to the way things are ordained.

It helps immeasurably to recognize that doctors and nurses are devoted to the task of making us well again. They do not enjoy our ailments any more than we do. Their satisfaction comes from our healing. Nurses may have bad days now and then, days when they are brusque and out of sorts. So do we all. Doctors may be thoughtless or preoccupied at times. They have their moods and occasionally they leave us anxious and lonely because they are in a hurry and tell us less than they might to encourage us. Fundamentally, however, they are genuinely concerned about us.

One cold, gloomy Sunday afternoon, visiting in a hospital, I met a doctor in the elevator. He smiled and remarked, "On days like this I try to see my patients. They always feel poorly on dark days and I usually can brighten the day for them." He did brighten their days with encouragement. He really cared. So do most of the many doctors I have known. As a group they go far beyond the call of duty to help those entrusted to their care.

More often than not our problem is ourselves, our attitudes and our anxieties. The truth is suggested by the fact that two patients having the same doctors and nurses in the same hospital with the same illness react differently to hospital routine. One of the two says the meals are terrible, the nurses inefficient, and the hospital below par. He is quite certain the doctor does not know his business. The other of the two says the food is excellent, the nurses wonderful, and the doctors "tops." He is cheerful and full of hope for the future. What is more, he is making an excellent recovery while the other, gloomy and pessimistic, is not doing well.

Doctors and nurses often are frustrated by patients they want to help. They are irritated by those who are full of complaint and inconsiderate of others. They are annoyed by the self-centeredness of those who are forever clamoring for attention whether needed or not. Of course, the more disagreeable the patient, the more he is avoided. On the other hand, there are uncomplaining, thoughtful patients who are literally overwhelmed by the kindness of nurses and hospital attendants. As one nurse said of a gracious patient, "She is a joy to serve." Obviously, it is the disagreeable patients who are lonely and left alone.

Clearly, our anxieties and our moods have much to do with the way we feel about hospitals, doctors, and nurses. There are those who decide before they register at the admitting office that their experience will be distasteful and unpleasant: the room will be too hot or too cold, the hospital personnel will be indifferent, and so on. If they decide on a private room they will be lonely. If they choose a double room they are persuaded the roommate will be annoying. Whatever they do they will wish they had done something else.

The average patient is in a state of emotional turmoil when he enters the hospital. He is disposed to be quarrelsome and difficult because he is full of fears. Doctors and nurses are tolerant and understanding. They are acutely aware of the patient's apprehensions and they seek to reassure him. Nevertheless, it is difficult to argue with an emotion. Logic usually comes off second best when our inner feelings are involved. So, patients are likely to be on edge, and the ordeal of tests and examinations does little to calm their anxieties.

Several things should be noted when we are faced with the prospect of going to the hospital. The first is that hospitalization does not necessarily mean we are on the road to an untimely end. More and more doctors are sending patients to hospitals as preventive measures. With Blue Cross and various forms of hospital insurance, we go to healing institutions more readily than in the past. We go for treatment of minor ailments and for tests to make sure nothing serious is in the offing.

If surgery is required the chances are we will be home in a week or two. Surgery is not the hazardous venture of twenty-five years ago before modern techniques and drugs became available. Most operations today are routine, involving a couple of days of real discomfort and a few days for primary healing. Thereafter, rest and a reasonable routine will restore us to health.

There are times, of course, when we face serious problems,

hazardous operations, and an uncertain future. We need to be mindful, then, that the surgeon, the nurses, and other participants in the enterprise on our behalf are men and women of competence and integrity. In the recovery room they will watch over us twenty-four hours a day. I have seen doctors stand by a patient all night, giving more of themselves than anyone has a right to expect. I have seen nurses ministering without thought of themselves to make patients comfortable.

We may feel like ciphers, bogged down in hospital beds, but it is not really so. On the contrary, we are very important people to those who care for us. We can make their tasks very difficult or we can make them simpler, depending on our willingness to cooperate and to be considerate. What is more, the doctor who seemed casual may turn out to be the soul of helpfulness, and the nurse who appeared a "sour puss" may in fact be wonderfully efficient and kind.

A long stint in the hospital requires considerable patience. We wish we could be anywhere except where we are. Heart patients who often feel fit after a week or so resent the necessity for staying in bed six or eight weeks. They fret and fume and so hinder the healing process. But if they relax and accept necessity they discover that a hospital room is not really unpleasant. Books and magazines become a resource and rest a boon to a tired body. What is more, if they obey the doctor's orders and change their pace when they are back in circulation again they are likely to live to a ripe old age.

WAITING IN TRUST

Nothing, I am sure, is more important in the healing process than the grace of acceptance and relaxed surrender. When we accept the fact that we are dependent on the competence and care of others and on the healing grace of God and stop protesting, a gentle conspiracy of nature, human compassion, and God take over for our good. When we give up trying to manage our own cases and relax in trust all the resources of nature and God rally to our defense. We literally commit suicide with protest and tension; we are saved by surrender.

Protest and resentment against illness keep God at a distance and isolate us from those who wish to be helpful. Catherine Marshall observed wisely concerning a long illness she suffered that day after day she lay incapacitated in protest. She prayed for healing and help. She felt exasperated when God did not answer her prayers. The longer her illness continued the more she was irritated by it. It was not right. It was not fair. She had a family to care for and work to do. She kept herself in a state of exhaustion protesting against her illness. Then, one day, she gave up, and prayed in simple humility, "Dear God, use me any way you please." Curiously, in the very moment she ceased to protest, her healing began. Quite literally, she opened the door to God's healing power.

George Fox somewhere described a woman who had been ill for a long period. She was resentful and full of protest, feeling that God had wronged her. Evidently Fox knew her well and visited her often. When she had recovered he commented cryptically, "God settled her mind and she mended." Often we have to wait in trust for God to settle our minds before we can be mended. What is more, God waits for us to surrender in trust before He can settle our minds.

Frequently in illness our minds are unsettled, not by protest and resentment, but by anxiety and feelings of inadequacy. We wonder if we have what it takes to cope with the future. We feel utterly alone facing dark and foreboding tomorrows without strength to carry on. Our weakness discounts our recuperative powers and makes us wonder whether we will be competent to do what we must in the days to come.

One woman suffering on a hospital bed unburdened herself by saying, "My husband needs somebody who is strong, able to care for the children and keep him going." Then she added, "Just look at me. I'm like a cobweb, easily torn and bruised." Her whole world seemed to have caved in, leaving her with a horrible sense of her own inadequacy. Why get well, she wondered, if she could not carry her load?

Or, there was the man of forty-six, trying to recover from a severe heart condition. "I'm through so far as a business promotion is concerned," he said plaintively. "How can I pull my weight if I always have to remember I have to save myself?" His aspirations and dreams had come to an end in the painful realization of his limitations. In his despair he thought he might as well be dead.

We always exaggerate our feelings of inadequacy when we are ill and seldom consider the resources with which we may cope with our limitations. We feel somewhat like the man driving an old truck, trying to pull a heavy load of wood up a steep mountain road. The water in the truck radiator was boiling and the motor was on the verge of stalling. It appeared that the truck was going to stall at any moment. There was no power in reserve, nothing left for a steeper pitch. As I watched, it occurred to me that a good many people I know are precisely like the man in the truck. They have nothing in reserve. They are pulling all they can manage. Any extra strain would break them. Somewhere, somehow, they need to find new resources to keep them going. They cannot run out from under the loads they are pulling and they cannot keep on without new strength. It is God or collapse for them, as Marjorie Lawrence discovered when polio struck her down. "Truly the Lord is my strength and song, and has become my salvation,"[5] she wrote after she had fought her way back from despair and defeat.

The presence and the power of God are by no means figments of the imagination. They carry us through the valleys and the shadows of illness to the sunlit slopes on the other side. Day after day we pray, "Thine is the power," and we are adequate for anything if we believe it.

MEANING IN PAIN

We can endure suffering and make it pay a high rate of interest if we are able to make something of it for ourselves and others. It was Baron von Hügel, the great mystic, bearing his suffering with grace and courage, who noted that the greatest trial of suffering is the seeming futility of it. It is suffering for nothing, enduring pain to no good end that hurts us most. The G.I. in Korea, feeling the pain of hurt friends, was overwhelmed with bitterness because, as he saw it, "This war is stupid nonsense." He could not see the wider hope of peace beyond the mountains of Korea, or feel that any good could come from all the pain he saw. There is, of course, the grim chance he may have been right, and yet he gave voice to an essential truth, namely, that suffering to be endured must be meaningful. We cannot endure pain that is sheer nonsense.

Admiral Byrd, utterly alone and ill, suffering intensely in a lonely outpost on Little America, found his pain endurable for two reasons. He was an instrument of the truth, pushing back the frontiers of our knowledge of the snowy wastes, and quite unexpectedly in his suffering aloneness he found God and knew he was not alone. There was meaning in his pain, and like John Milton, he found it quite possible to "justify the ways of God to man."

The pain of pioneers had meaning as they pushed across the plains. They were instruments for "the taming of the West." The agony of those who pushed toward Mount Everest's crest could be faced with high courage, for suffering was the price brave men paid for conquest of the heights. Mothers do not deeply mind the pain of birth because through pain new life is wrought. The pain is incidental to the life that is to be, a trial whose end is triumph. But the pain that is only pain, whose end is still more pain, is something else again. It seems so sterile, so utterly useless. It creates nothing. It builds nothing. To suffer for the sake of something yet to be is a sacred grace; to suffer for nothing is a devastating hell. As the old Negro spiritual has it, "You gotta get a glory" from whatever comes to you. If there is no meaning, no glory in the suffering we endure, life falters and the spirit fails.

Mankind has tried quite endlessly to come to terms with suffering. The Stoics tried the hopeless little game of denying the reality of pain. It was only an illusion, which the Stoic mind would master. The optimists in various guises declare that suffering is good in disguise (which it never is), and the pessimists find in pain a bulwark for their contention that the world is altogether evil. Suffering is food for their brooding melancholy. Jesus, on the other hand, faced suffering quite honestly. He did not call it good. He tried neither to explain it nor to explain it away. He insisted, however, that suffering could become a means of grace and inner power, a doorway into the presence of God Himself.

Unless we are altogether blind we shall see in our own

experience clear evidence of God's love in suffering. Let a beloved child be stricken by accident or illness and life takes on a different hue. What was important yesterday is not important today. Our sense of values is completely changed. The conflicts of our homes are stilled and our families draw together. A gentle conspiracy of friendship gathers around us, and we feel the warmth of human compassion that, in truth, seems more than human. Strength and dignity overflow from nowhere we can fathom, and "deep calleth unto deep." Our child's suffering is not futile, nor is it sterile if these gifts are ours. John Gunther understood the truth when the suffering and death of his only son brought unity to his broken home and opened doors to God that had been altogether closed before.

But there is yet a deeper note that sounds in our experience when suffering claims a child. The floodgates of our compassion are opened wide. Love, tenderness, and devotion overwhelm us, and we come as close to the child as life can come to life. What is more, there is response, as if our love and strength had summoned faith and courage from the buried depths of pain. In a way we cannot explain, the child borrows from an undiscovered store of quietness in us and feels a steady trust that all is well when we are by his side. Together, in our oneness, we can manage anything that comes. It is suffering that brings us as close to a child as life can come to life, or soul can come to soul. Our strength is made perfect in a child's weakness.

To be sure, human analogies never are altogether adequate, and yet, in suffering God comes as close to us as life can come to life. God is love, love that shares and divides the poignancy of pain. God is love, love that shares its strength, lends a healing touch, and breathes the benediction of unfailing peace. Suffering is by no means futile if from its depth we hear the voice of the Eternal saying to us as it said to Paul: "My grace is sufficient for thee, for my power is made perfect in weakness."[6]

POWER FROM AFFLICTION

Of course, there is no assurance that we will touch some trail of the garment of God in the hours of our lonely suffering. There is no certainty that our pain will lift our horizons and let us see the living God. We can choose to be blind, blind to the love of God and unmindful of the grace that lifts. We can choose to be blind to the possibilities hidden in the soul of suffering until pain becomes utterly without meaning, a blank wall of unrelieved anguish. But if our eyes are open toward God, we can find meaning in our pain and make it significant for great enduring and great living.

"Before I was afflicted I went astray: but now I keep thy word,"[7] was the Psalmist's way of saying that by way of suffering he came to know the goodness of God. "Thou art good and doest good,"[8] he wrote through the pain of his affliction. "Teach me good judgment and knowledge."[9] His affliction was not futile. It left him with insight, faith, and a new sense of values. The writer of Hebrews remarks sagely of Jesus: "Although he was a Son, he learned obedience through what he suffered."[10] The meaning of suffering for the Psalmist was determined by the values he wrested from it, and the significance of the suffering of Jesus is to be found in the creative power that came out of it. The Cross of Calvary is the deepest symbol there is of the suffering of God, God on a cross, but the significance of God's suffering is to be found in the creative power that flowed from it; power to transform life, to make saints of sinners, to build a church and alter the face of the earth.

To be sure, suffering in itself has no power to alter life. Cancer and polio, sorrow and heartache are morally neutral. They are powerless to make us either saints or cynics, wise or foolish. Milk and flour, butter and eggs have no power to make a cake, they are but ingredients for the creative mind to use. Without that creative mind they turn sour, rancid, and useless. Suffering is powerless to create knowledge and insight, courage and goodness until it is touched by the creative mind of God in us. But the grace of God in us can transform our suffering into an inner glory.

Lord Byron and Sir Walter Scott both were sufferers, but they found very different meanings in their suffering. To Byron it meant bitterness and frustration that made him, as his biographer notes, "both cynical and savage." It was quite otherwise with Sir Walter Scott. Neither suffering nor debt could spoil his life nor cramp his soul with meanness. Instead, he opened his eyes to God. His life was radiant and through all his novels there runs a note of triumph. "He learned . . . through what he suffered" and his pen gave voice to insight wrought in pain.

Years ago I used to visit a little girl whose body had been wasted by a strange affliction. You would think she would be bitter, resentful that life had passed her by and left her helpless on her bed. You would think to see her there would be more tears than laughter in her life. But it was not so. She saw more of God from her bedroom window than most of us see in a lifetime of walking and traveling about. She sang more from her bed than most of us ever sing. The thought of her is a tonic in discouragement, a benediction in despair. The simple poetry she composed and recited is shining testimony to the richness of her quiet faith in life and God.

Clearly, we decide the meaning we shall give to our suffering and determine the significance it shall have for our lives. But in the end, what our suffering means, whether it is creative or utterly destructive, depends upon whether we choose to be blind or whether we choose to see God in the gentle conspiracy of love and mercy that gathers around us.

AN INVITATION TO TRIUMPH

It is a strange fact that in the logic of God there is a correlation between suffering and greatness. A South Indian proverb has it that, "He who is born in the fire will not fade in the sun," as if life needed to be tempered in order to withstand "the destruction that wasteth at noonday." The "valley of the shadow" is a vale of soul-making. Tragedy is an invitation to triumph; suffering the summons to sovereignty; and pain the call to power. Any lover of poetry knows that there is a somber note of pain at the heart of all great poetry; and any lover of music knows that there is a note of tragedy in all of our greatest music.

Isaiah felt the truth when he wrote of greatness in terms of suffering and painted in words the sublime picture of "the suffering servant" of mankind. He was "wounded for our transgressions; he was bruised for our iniquities."[11] "He was oppressed, and he was afflicted."[12] Nevertheless, "with his stripes are we healed."[13] So, it is the sufferers who heal us by their insights, inspire us by their courage, lift us by their creative powers. It is no accident that Tennyson's greatest poem was inspired by the suffering and the death of his friend Arthur Hallam. In all suffering "deep calleth unto deep," and we are invited to greatness of mind and spirit.

One of the astonishing discoveries of one who reads biography is that those who achieved greatness did it in spite of something that led them to suffer. Alexander Pope was deformed. His biographer says he "inherited nothing from his father except his deformity and nothing from his mother but her violent headaches." Little more than four feet in height, his bodily infirmities rendered his life one long disease. Nevertheless, he added glorious pages to English literature. Lord Kelvin, the great scientist, was a cripple and so was Louis Pasteur. Keats and Emerson, Sidney Lanier and Katherine Mansfield were afflicted with tuberculosis. They were suffering servants of mankind, whose suffering God transformed into greatness. Of all such men and women we can say: "With his stripes are we healed."

Paul Scherer tells the story of a friend who came asking the age-old question about suffering. "Why does God allow it?" he wanted to know. Then without waiting for an answer he went on: "I have seen a captain send one of his men, a dear friend of his, to certain death; and the man spent no time in asking why. He saluted and went. I do not know why, and I am not asking. I am just saluting, if that is my part. In God's name, can't we have the courage even of soldiers? He knows. So much I understand."

Somehow the great sufferers have saluted, marched on in lonely grandeur with the mystery of their suffering, and found the "strength" that is "made perfect in weakness." They have had the courage of soldiers and more, and in God's grace they have marched to triumph with their eyes open, fixed upon the hills of God, from whence comes their strength.

Such was the mood of Robert Louis Stevenson. There is a famous portrait of Stevenson, propped up in bed, with the counterpane drawn up over his shrunken knees, playing the flute. He would play his flute and write his immortal stories for "Christ's sake," pain or no pain. He would cheer his more fortunate but despairing friends. He would do what he loved most of all to do—live richly in his own mind and heart. As one of his friends said of him, he had the "determination to win an honorable discharge in the bankrupt business of human life." But more, he had an unrelenting purpose: a determination to prove what God can do with a bankrupt body inspired by a faithful soul.

So, as George Matheson noted in the midst of his blindness, it is necessary in all affliction "to pass from the life of the egotist to the life of the humanitarian," from self-concern to other concern. What matters, really, is not what happens to us, but what happens to others because of us. If we fail, what will others think of our faith? If we are weak, how will others view our beliefs? If we go to pieces, what will others think of our Christ? But if we take the worst in our stride and make music, won't others want what we have? If we glorify God with courage and hope and undiscouraged cheerfulness, all that happens to us may well turn out "unto the progress of the gospel." It will be clear to all that God has said to us as He said to Paul, "My grace is sufficient for thee, for my power is made perfect in weakness."[14]

Give Me Your Tears

T HE "valley of the shadow of death" is another of life's inevitabilities. Sooner or later we trudge through it ourselves to meet our
destiny beyond. Perhaps more poignant is the fact we may be
called upon to journey through the valley beside someone we
have loved deeply, a wife or husband, a son or a daughter. That,
more often than not, is a supreme test of our faith and of our
spiritual maturity.

BEREAVEMENT

Our problem is: how do we cope with our aloneness? How do
we face the days without being overwhelmed by our grief? The
dreams and hopes we shared gave meaning to our lives, and
shared memories, both happy and sad, enriched our comradeship.
We know what Goethe meant when he exclaimed on learning of
the death of his cherished friend, Karl August, "Now nothing
remains." In our grief we are sure nothing remains but a lonely
and meaningless journey on through the years.

We are a little resentful not only because we have been left
alone but also because if our loved ones cherished life and
anticipated the future, we feel as if they had been cheated of
what Browning's Rabbi Ben Ezra called "The last of life, for
which the first was made." We wish they could have gone on to
see the fulfillment of their hopes and plans. We know how much
they wanted to enjoy the sunset years, doing things they never
had time to do in the years of struggle and getting ahead.

Often we are able to manage the initial shock of loss with what might be called "cornered courage." We rise to the occasion and travel through, supported by friends and neighbors. We shed tears without shame and everyone understands. But then comes the loneliness, the feeling of isolation and inability to think of anything except our loss. J. Middleton Murry spoke for the legions of the bereaved when he wrote after the death of his wife, Katherine Mansfield, that he felt isolated in spirit "as a little island whose slender shores the cold, dark, boundless ocean lapped devouring."

Sometimes on our little island we experience feelings of guilt. We know that through the years we might have been more thoughtful, more considerate. We wish we had been at our best, day in and day out, through all the years that are gone. We could have avoided the conflict and many of the tensions that marred the years. Why, oh why did we say hard things we really did not mean? Why did we fly off in anger the way we did? Our aloneness would be more tolerable if it were not for what we feel in retrospect were our own failures.

Grief is endlessly multiplied by regret. Thomas Carlyle, remembering his unkindness to his wife, Jane, condemned himself bitterly and wrote, "She was the sunshine of my poor, dripping days," and his sorrow was intensified by his regret. He felt depressed and unworthy, full of self-condemnation.

So, in our self-condemnation we feel depressed and gloomy, and feeling thus we are inclined to withdraw from our normal activities. One woman expressed her feeling by saying, "I don't want to depress other people, so I stay home." And, alone at home, she remained inert and unutterably sad. There was, it seemed to her, no sorrow like her sorrow, and no loss equal to hers.

It would help immeasurably if we could know when we lose loved ones that these feelings, in varying degrees, are common to all who "walk through the valley of the shadow of death" with loved ones. The "cornered courage" of the moment of shock, the sense of isolation and feelings of guilt and depression are normal for us all in times of grief. There may be some hositility and bitterness, too, and the resentful question, "Why should this happen to me?" All these are quite human.

Peril lies not in feeling as we do, but in prolonged withdrawal from life, in our refusal to adjust to reality. There are those who incur the judgment of Dante, as having "wilfully lived in sadness," unwilling to accept life on the terms that are common to all mankind. We need to remember that there are, as Vergil said, "tears in things." Indeed, the epigram of Palladas of Alexandria in his Greek *Anthology* might be made to summarize the experience of the race:

> Tears were my birthright; born in tears,
> In tears too must I die;
> And mine has been, through life's long years
> A tearful destiny.[1]

Grief treads on the heels of grief in life and we cannot escape from "the tears in things."

HONEST TEARS

Under the stress of grief, weeping is not a sign of weakness. On the contrary, there are honest tears of which we need not be ashamed. It is unfortunate, I think, that men have been conditioned not to show their grief. Dr. Granger Westberg remarks that when a little boy falls and skins his knee and cries out in pain, someone picks him up and says, "Now, now, little man, don't cry. Be a man." And when he is eight years old and hurts himself, he does not dare cry, nor at eighteen when something happens about which he ought to cry. At thirty-eight when some great loss is suffered, he cannot cry.

We sometimes think that letting ourselves go emotionally might lead to a "nervous breakdown." The truth is quite otherwise. It is the individual who holds himself tense, who refuses to let go, who may be in for trouble. The Scriptures suggest plainly that when great sorrow came to hardy men of faith they wept bitterly, their "tears like a torrent day and night."[2]

To be sure, we need not overdo what is essentially a good thing. It is good to express whatever grief we really feel, and we do not need to be ashamed. The pain we feel at the moment is the tool and instrument of our later healing. Nevertheless, grief that is legitimate at its beginning may, if prolonged, impair recovery of spirit. While it is normal for anyone to be plunged into grief by the death of a beloved, it is by no means a sign of emotional health to be so permanently inconsolable that he retreats from the human enterprise.

Years ago I used to visit an elderly widow whose husband had died twenty years before. In all those years she had kept her husband's room precisely as it was the day he died. His clothes still hung in the closet and his toothbrush and razor were in the bathroom cabinet. When her husband died, the woman simply resigned from the human enterprise and seldom emerged from the gloom of her home. There was no rejoicing in her heart, no understanding of the words, "I will see you again."

The old slogan of the theater, "The show must go on," is pertinent. We have no choice but to go on despite grief if we are emotionally mature. It is significant that after the resurrection Jesus appeared to His disciples at the Sea of Galilee. They were distraught, defeated, and crushed. To Peter, Jesus said, "Do you love me?" and when Peter answered, "Lord, . . . you know that I love you," Jesus responded by saying, "Feed my sheep."[3] So, to retreat from life in grief is not evidence of love. On the contrary, love is evident in carrying on. We honor those we have loved not by prolonged and inconsolable grief, but rather by pushing on with creativity and with faith.

Reading the story of Acts, it is clear that the disciples did not begin to rejoice or to live creatively until they began to answer the summons, "Feed my sheep." They lost sight of themselves in their mission, and in serving His cause their hearts rejoiced. It is instructive, too, to discover that the disciples compensated for their regret by the way they met their grief. In serving as they did, they found forgiveness. Day by day they toiled, risked their lives for His sake, believing they would see Him again.

There is a collection of short stories by Tillie Olsen called *Tell Me a Riddle*. One story is of an old gentleman whose wife is dying. He listens to his wife's whisper, "Lost, how much I lost," and then to the climactic words, "there was joy, too." That is life, so much that is lost, missed on the road, and yet there is joy, too.

FACING UP TO LOSS

We ought to begin, then, with the cross in our common life, with "the tears in things." Like the New Testament, we need to admit that grief is an inescapable affair and face it. It is not wisdom to bury our heads in the sand, like the ostrich, and pretend our grief does not exist. It is not heroism to continue on as if nothing had happened. When, like Jacob, we are "left alone," we have no choice except to face our aloneness and come to terms with it. Heroes do not run away from life; they live it to the fullest. To try to avoid the pain of grief is to find temporary relief, only to suffer more deeply as the rolling years move on. Nothing is settled until it is settled right.

Thanks chiefly to the psychiatrist Erich Lindemann and his colleagues at the Massachusetts General Hospital we have begun to learn something about the human response to bereavement and the ways men and women react to the loss of loved ones. Dr. Lindemann's study began at the time of the catastrophic Cocoa-nut Grove fire in Boston, when many of the injured survivors were brought to the hospital. Nearly all of them had lost husbands or wives, sweethearts, intimate friends, or close relatives. The surgical department, troubled because the burns of many patients were not healing, sought the aid of psychiatrists.

Dr. Lindemann wisely studied both those whose burns were healing normally and those whose healing was delayed. When he examined the feelings and attitudes of those who were making rapid medical progress, he discovered there was a remarkable correlation between the "grief reactions" of patients and their medical progress. Those who were making rapid medical progress were facing up to their loss. They were disposed to relive their tragic experience, often with great mental pain. They remembered what they had been doing with the beloved just before the tragedy struck. They recalled their hurt, their fright, the last moments of the fire, and all the vivid details of it. When the pain of recollection was too great, they turned from it. Often they recalled memories from the past. They thought of the life they had shared with their beloved, the joys they had known together.

Some of the sufferers carried through the process of recollection on their own, others wanted to talk with someone about the past and the tragedy itself. But in every case, those who were able to reconstruct and relive both the tragedy and the past were able to deal with their grief, and were able to consider the remaking of their lives on the basis of the new situation. Their burns healed quickly.

Those whose burns healed slowly had quite different responses. Some were resentful and rebellious. Others were sentimental. Still others maintained a stiff upper lip and exhibited little emotion. Some locked their feelings inside and shed no tears. But they all had one thing in common. They were unable to confront openly the stark pain which would come if they faced up to the reality and the full implications of their loss.[4]

There is something for all of us here, an obvious suggestion that we had best face and admit honestly "the tears in things." Do not run away from grief. Face it relentlessly, the loss, the pain, the loneliness. Feel what you ought to feel. Think it out and talk it out until you are free to face life and deal with it triumphantly. God cannot enter to "wipe away all tears" until you face your grief bluntly and measure the implications of it.

ACCEPTING GRIEF

There is a corollary, then, to the suggestion that grief must be faced, and the corollary is that grief must be accepted. Those who were resentful and rebellious after the Cocoanut Grove fire, found their own healing thwarted and delayed. It is so in our common experience. Triumphant spiritual healing after tragedy or loss is delayed and thwarted when we resent our hurt and retreat into bitterness.

How easy it is to nurse "bitter thoughts" when those who are dearest to us slip from our grasp. But in bitterness there is no healing and no help.

Among the parables of Buddha is the account of a woman who lost an only son. She was grief-stricken beyond reason. She went from house to house asking for medicine to relieve her agony. At last she went to Buddha who said he could cure her with a few grains of mustard seed if she would bring them to him. One stipulation was that the mustard seed must come from a home in which no one had lost a child, a husband, parent, or dear friend.

She went from house to house, but in every case she found some loved one had been lost.

Having traveled through the neighborhood, the grief-stricken mother began to understand her grief was not unique. "How selfish I am in my grief," she said to herself. Then, coming to terms with reality, she said to herself, "Death is common to all; yet in this valley of desolation there is a path that leads him to immortality who has surrendered all selfishness." So, in grief, *we* are the problem until we accept reality and surrender the selfishness that keeps us in our gloom.

That is not to say, of course, that we should treat loss with casualness, or feel no pain. We never altogether escape the poignancy of loss, nor do we wish to do so. There is, for those who have loved deeply, a continual freshness of loss even after years. But there also is acceptance, the relaxation of protest, and renewal of the patterns of our lives. A dear friend whose small son was killed in an accident, and who carried through the agony with grace and acceptance, said thoughtfully, "There are times when memory stabs me like a sharp knife. It may happen on a bright day in the woods, or when I am at work in my office."

We all know something of that experience, and it is not that we willfully live in sadness. But love twines its way into our hearts and minds and the memory of a cherished comradeship keeps coming back not simply to plague us and to make us miserable but rather to remind us, as Tennyson said, that "It is better to have loved and lost, then never to have loved at all."[5]

When we accept reality with its grief and loss and push on, we do so with deeper insight and larger creativity. It was so in the experience of Käthe Kollwitz, a German artist whose life and art were one. Many of her subjects were drawn from her husband's medical clinic, and he hardly ministered to their bodies more than she ministered to the spirits of many of his patients. Her greatest work came about through the death of a son during World War I, and her graphic creations became a memorial to the suffering and misfortune in the lives she knew. Tragedy gave depth and wider meaning to her creations.

It is in "the valley of the shadow of death" that we expand the dimensions of our lives if we are able to accept reality and come to terms with it. The world's greatest poetry has come from the valley of the shadow, and so has the world's greatest art. The noblest contributors to the common life of mankind have been great sufferers who made the acceptance of their grief the touchstone of their power. What is more, many of the most gracious and self-effacing men and women I have known have been those who endured great loss.

We have a choice, you and I, when we meet "the tears in things." We can go on through the years, living in "willful sadness," protesting in bitterness, shrouding the world in gloom, or, on the other hand, we can accept reality and make our grief creative.

ACCEPTANCE OF REALITY

The simple and inescapable truth is that nobody can get through to help us find our way until we do accept reality. Not even God can break through the egocentric trap of self-pity and protest until we surrender our selfishness and come to terms with things as they are. In our grief we are somewhat in the predicament of the alcoholic who cannot be helped by anyone until he accepts the fact he is an alcoholic and then seeks help. It is then that other people and God can break through his defenses against life, sustain and help him.

What is more, it is the recovered alcoholic, reaching out with understanding and compassion born of his own experience, who is able to help another in need of help. He speaks and shares from the depths of his own memory, from insight born in the agony of his own inebriation and haunting regret. And in the same fashion one who has suffered bereavement and loss is able to get through the defenses of one burdened by grief. There is between them a fellowship of pain and shared experience.

Job, the suffering patriarch, his children dead, found little help in those who had "made an appointment together to come to condole with him and comfort him."[6] Their efforts to help by reliving Job's experience with him and looking for an explanation of it were so unsuccessful that the term "Job's comforters" has become proverbial for those whose sympathy only serves to intensify distress. The reason for the failure of Job's friends is simple. What Job needed was not argument and platitudes, but sympathetic understanding.

It is important to notice that in the early portions of the drama, Job had not accepted reality. He was in a state of protest, even against God. "I would argue with the Lord," he said. "Why do you play dirty tricks on me?" is the essence of Job's protest to God. But there came a moment when, in the words of the dramatist, "The Lord spoke to Job out of the whirlwind," and in a magnificent response Job accepted reality, saying, "I had heard of thee by the hearing of the ear, but now my eye sees thee."[7]

Apparent throughout the drama of Job, is the fact God is waiting in the wings for Job to accept the reality of his situation and deal with it creatively and in faith. There is a hint of what I mean in Tillie Olsen's *Tell Me a Riddle,* in which one of the characters, in spite of loneliness and fear, pain and betrayal, says in the spirit of acceptance, "There still is enough left to live by." Job found it so, and so do we all.

Indeed, in the maturity of our acceptance of reality we find strength and dignity and capacity to enter creatively into the lives of other sufferers with whom we find fellowship. They get through to us and we to them, and in our understanding communion we find God.

STRENGTH FOR OUR WEAKNESS

So it is that the New Testament promises comfort to the grief-stricken. Notice the word "comfort." It comes from two Latin words, *con* and *fortis.* Literally the combination means "strengthened by being with." So, comfort is not a sentimental affair. It is a reinforcing of the heart with strength and courage from the spiritual depths of life. "God shall wipe away all tears" by reinforcing life and bearing it onward.

Seward Hiltner aptly describes the spiritual reinforcing of life in his story of the woman of middle years whose son was a Nazi prisoner during the Second World War. Knowing her honesty and her fortitude, Dr. Hiltner asked, "How do you feel about it?" She replied, "I'm scared to death." Then she added, paradoxically, "But I'm not afraid." Wisely she acknowledged her fear and torment, aware that her inner life was deeply touched; and yet, she also had found a holy of holies in the depths of herself. In that inner sanctuary she was not afraid. There she found calmness and strength to see her through.

That is our task: to acknowledge our grief and our hurt and yet to have an inner holy of holies where we find refuge and courage in the comradeship of Jesus Christ. There is light for our darkness and strength for our weakness, for we are not alone. As a lovely old Jewish hymn has the truth:

> Every tear on earth that flows,
> God the ruler surely knows.[8]

That is the affirmation of the Christian faith, made regnant on a cross. God is in the midst of our suffering and grief, not to explain it, but to share it.

Not long ago in visiting with a courageous woman whose husband had been ill for more than a year, I remarked that through it all she had been a "good soldier." "Oh," she answered, "God has been my strength." Then she went on to say: "God works in strange ways. There were times when I thought I could not go on. Then the telephone would ring and somebody on the other end of the line would give me a needed lift. Or, maybe the doorbell would ring, and there would be someone I did not expect to see. Or, perhaps it would be a letter of encouragement. There were other times when I just picked up my Bible or repeated the Twenty-third Psalm."

Curiously, I never had thought of the woman in question as particularly religious, but there she was telling me that God had had a hand in the telephone calls that came at precisely the right moment and the ringing of the doorbell and the letters. There she was telling me God led her to the Scriptures and that in the deepest possible sense her prayers had been answered.

How blind we often are! Time and again in my ministry I have had a curious feeling I ought to go see somebody. There seemed to be no good reason for going, but I have learned to listen to those hunches. When I have gone I have found the reason for going, illness or trouble of one sort or another. Call my hunches what you will, I am altogether sure God has a hand in them. I am sure He has a hand in your strange feelings you ought to go here or there to be helpful.

God is mindful of the tears that flow, and in a hundred ways He comes to share the hurt. He comes through the ministry of others and He comes to the inner sanctuary. When He comes, we are not afraid.

That leads to the observation that when our grief is faced and accepted, the resources of the spirit bring strength to transform it. There is a hint of what I mean in the words engraved on a plaque in historic King's Chapel in Boston. It is on the box-pew of "Theodore Pickering, Litt. D. One who could share in the whole world's tears, And still be glad."

Theodore Pickering was born during the dark years of the Civil War; his death came during the period of World War I. He must have been a sensitive man to be described as sharing the whole world's tears. More than once his spirit must have been depressed as the sorrows and hurts of his generation overflowed upon him. And, I dare say, his compassion and his capacity to "share in the whole world's tears" came from some personal loss of his own. It always is so.

As Karl Barth noted, "The generation that has no great anguish on its heart will have no great music on its lips." So, the man or woman who bears no great anguish of the heart will have no great song to sing. Paradoxically, it is "the tears in things" that in the end beget the power to "still be glad." It is the tears in life that breed compassion and understanding. It was the tears in the life of Walt Whitman that begot his sympathy for all mankind. The tears of God, watching while they crucified His son, begot redemptive power.

It is God who speaks to us in our grief:

> Bring me, when dancers leave the hall,
> Your aching heart.
> Give other friends your lighted face,
> The laughter of the years.
> I come to crave a greater grace,
> Bring me your tears.[9]

And, having brought our aching hearts to the foot of the Cross of Christ, "God shall wipe away all tears" and leave us "still glad."

So we need not be afraid of the dark clouds with which life overshadows us, because we know we always find God in them. A chaplain, during World War II, painted a picture in words of the heroism and courage of American G.I.'s. In the tenseness of the dark night before an attack, he was ministering to the wounded and the dying, praying with the reconnaissance groups before they began picking at mine fields, riding in an ambulance over a dangerous bridge after a night burial, and throughout all these events there was one recurring theme, expressed as his book's title, *And God Was There*. In the black clouds of doubt, uncertainty, fear, suffering, and death, God was there.

We would expect God where there is lightheartedness and joy, and of course He is there. We wonder sometimes if He is in "the valley of the shadow," and yet it is in the valleys of weeping that we have our most intimate communion with God. He comes to us from the heart of a cross, understanding the agony of grief, and saying, "Lo, I am with you always."[10] Again and again and again when I have shared the grief of men and women, I have been aware of God lending His strength and His grace to those in the valley.

I cannot explain what I know, nor can anyone else. Christ crucified was "a stumbling block to Jews and folly to Gentiles,"[11] and a suffering God seems a far cry from the sovereign Lord of the universe. And yet, it is the compassionate God who has shared and still shares our pain and hurt who gets through to us in our grief. We cannot put the explanation into words, but we know the experience. When Isaac Newton's claim to the discovery of calculus was challenged, someone sent him a problem that could not be solved without it. He returned the solution the next day. That was enough. It is enough for us to know that the God of the cross is our God and that in His strength we are able for anything.

THOU ART WITH ME

God does not leave us in despair and loneliness. He comes to us in the light of an Easter dawn and, as Tennyson wrote,

O, yet we trust that somehow good
Will be the final goal of ill,

. . . .

That nothing walks with aimless feet;
That not one life shall be destroy'd,
Or cast as rubbish to the void,
When God hath made the pile complete.

. . . .

Behold, we know not anything;
I can but trust that good shall fall
At last—far off—at last, to all,
And every winter change to spring.[12]

So, "though I walk through the valley of the shadow of death, I fear no evil; for Thou art with me."[13]

10

Creative Solitude

THE DICTIONARY makes very little distinction between loneliness and solitude. To be lonely is "to stand apart from others," to be "isolated," and "unhappy at being alone; longing for friends." Solitude is "the state of being solitary, or alone." It suggests being secluded, isolated, remote from others. The distinction seems to be one between tweedledee and tweedledum. Nevertheless, usage in literature suggests loneliness is more negative than solitude. We seek solitude while we would escape loneliness.

To be lonely is to be cheerlessly solitary, beset by brooding melancholy, constrained to seek company and human fellowship, and bereft of love that warms the spirit. There is more than a little dejection and depression in loneliness, and perhaps resentment at having to be alone. Loneliness hurts; solitude heals. Loneliness brings a pain in the heart; solitude yields a lift to the spirit. The former is like a starless night, gloomy and foreboding; the latter is like the beauty of a cloudless night with the sky festooned by the tiny lights of the Milky Way.

There are those whose loneliness is deadly and there are others whose solitude is creative. Some dwell in a "fellowless firmament" all draped in weeds, like a weeping willow tree, while others, like Henry Thoreau, find both peace and insight in isolation from the lonely crowd. No stranger to aloneness, John Milton could sing,

> In solitude
> What happiness, who can enjoy alone,
> Or all enjoying, what contentment find?[1]

William Cowper, on the other hand, felt the brooding weight of isolation and lamented,

> I am out of humanity's reach,
> I must finish my journey alone,
> Never hear the sweet music of speech;
> I start at the sound of my own.[2]

We are destined to be, in the final summing up, alone. We have little or no choice about it. We may be surrounded by friends and loved ones, and yet there is an essential aloneness of the self. No one else can feel precisely what I feel or think exactly as I think. When we are in love we say "two hearts beat as one," and in the object of our affection we seem to find our alter ego. We share richly, and in love both our joys and sorrows are multiplied. But, even in our most intimate moments, we are separate souls, still decisively alone.

Outside my window as I write is a gnarled and twisted pine tree. The valley winds have pushed its needles and its branches toward the east, and left it quite naked on the west. A broken branch protrudes from its ample trunk above the still sturdy branch where once a rope swing provided entertainment for a boy. Chickadees and nuthatches, pine siskins and tanagers, Baltimore orioles and juncos flit from branch to branch, and a saucy blue jay squawks from a perch above the rest.

Heaven only knows the history my lonely pine has seen. Once the Ute and Arapaho Indians roamed the valley. Pioneers passed this way, and John Fremont may have made his camp near by as he pushed westward over Kenosha Pass. Miners on their way to Leadville passed by on the once rocky road that led them to the diggings. Summers and winters came and went. The years were dry or wet. The winters were bitter cold and the snow and ice covered my pine. It stood alone, braced against the storms.

My pine tree is a symbol, I think, of life. To be sure, there are other trees on the mountain, each with its separate history as well as its shared memories. But my tree stands in lonely grandeur, different from every other tree on the mountain side, unique in its posture. No other tree ever felt quite the same wintry blast, knew the weight of a small boy's swing, sheltered the nest of a wren, or felt the light touch of a resting hummingbird in precisely the fashion of my tree.

Similarly, my life is unique and yours is unique. My memories are mine and yours are yours. We can share them, after a fashion, but the emotional tone is different. There is something about my experience I cannot share and something about your experience you cannot fully share. We are alone, you and I, at the deepest levels of our lives. There is a gulf between ourselves and others that can not be crossed. So it is that aloneness is a simple and inescapable fact of life.

In one way or another we are constrained to deal with our aloneness. It may be that we find it difficult to endure, fraught with pain and with melancholy. Certainly the loneliness of moderns is a disturbing fact that leaves us restlessly seeking some escape. One troubled woman said plaintively, "If I had to spend an evening alone I'd be a complete wreck."

Haunted by our separateness, we nevertheless seek an anodyne for loneliness in the company of other people. We cannot face the awesome reality of our aloneness. Carl Sandburg's account of what the last man on earth is reported to have said is indicative. Looking first in one direction and then in another, apprehensively, the lone remnant of our species cried in agony, "Where is everybody?"

The trouble is, as Francis Bacon noted, that "a crowd is not company." The crowd is lonely. The individuals in it are

Ships that pass in the night, and speak each other in passing,[3]

but the speaking is mechanical. There is no deep communion with a crowd and one may look in every direction over a sea of faces and still say piteously, "Where is everybody?" Where are those with whom we can share something of our thinking and feeling? Where are those who care? We crave company, not crowds. Yet, even in congenial company, we still remain alone.

Overwork often is a compensation for loneliness that has not found its way to creative solitude. Some of the loneliest men I know are the most successful. They toil through the day and bring their brief cases home at night. They can endure their aloneness only when they are able to lose themselves in their labor. They are lost when they have a little time on their hands, no work to save themselves from their sense of isolation. If they go out at night, often it is to a cocktail party where fellowship is superficial. They wish they could be back at their work.

There is no escape from the truth that at the core of our minds we are profoundly alone. We have a choice, therefore, between loneliness and solitude, between melancholy and depression, and the capacity to enjoy our own thoughts. As John Milton said, "solitude sometimes is best society." It is the most satisfying company if we have painted the nooks and crannies of our minds with great pictures and filled them with worthy memories. Nothing will come of nothing, and if our minds are vacant, devoid of philosophy and faith, solitude is poor society.

If we are able to enjoy the temper of our own thoughts we can enjoy our own company, and our aloneness means not loneliness, but solitude. A teacher of philosophy I recall fell ill and retired to a cottage close to the university he loved. Remembering his love of fellowship and the warmth of his spirit, we wondered how he would manage his early retirement. We need not have worried. His mind was too full of great thoughts and great ideas to make room for self-pity or lonely depression. Students made a pathway to his door, not for his sake, but for theirs. They found a man whose solitude was rich in wisdom and understanding, a source of quiet strength.

An elderly woman I knew, a retired grade-school teacher, told me one day she hoped to write a book on the theme, "Is Your Mind an Asset?" She died before the book came to flower, but I always wished she had lived to write the book. She insisted that her days never were lonely, despite the fact she lived alone in a little house in the suburbs of Chicago. Her mind was so full of a number of things, so nimble as she ranged over her experience and her knowledge, that her solitude was a satisfaction, not a source of lonely depression.

Is your mind an asset or a liability as you wrestle with the aloneness at the core of yourself?

BALANCING SOLITUDE AND SOCIETY

The fact that we are essentially alone at the center of our being does not minimize our need for fellowship. Solitude, unbroken by companionship, is more than most of us can endure. We cannot "Live Alone and Like It," despite arguments to the contrary. What is the use of great ideas, nurtured in solitude, if we cannot share them? What is the purpose of wisdom, wrought in the fires of experience, if we cannot use it for the sake of other men and women? A full mind needs to be tempered and renewed by rubbing against other minds.

Cicero once wrote an essay "On Friendship" in which he noted that if a man should ascend into heaven "and get a clear view of the natural order of the universe" he would find small pleasure or satisfaction in the spectacle of heavenly glories unless he "had someone to whom to tell what he had seen." Indeed, the satisfactions of knowledge and insight are multiplied by the possibility of sharing.

If there were times when William Cowper longed for "a lodge in some vast wilderness," far from the consuming crowd, he was equally in need of fellowship to nurture the insights of his solitude. It is so for all of us. If there are times when sociableness murders solitude, there also are times when solitude demands sociableness. We need upper rooms where we can be alone to meditate, but we also need fireside fellowship to keep our souls and minds alive. It was James Russell Lowell who wrote, "Solitude is as needful to the imagination as society is wholesome for character."

The recluse is a sad and lonely man whose attitudes and feelings are distorted by his lack of companionship. His opinions have no source for correction and modification. His feelings fester without the healing grace of sharing. His ways are never challenged by the company of others. Lonely and depressed, he has no surcease from the self-pity that engulfs his life. His aloneness is no virtue if there is nothing in it beyond aloneness.

It may be that in God's wisdom, He "gives the desolate a home to dwell in," to relieve our solitariness with fellowship. To be sure, we may be lonely at home, our communion with one another destroyed by conflict. On the other hand, there may be such gracious fellowship that we are enriched and blessed by each other. Our solitude is warmed by the knowledge of the caring comradeship we know. Jessie Rittenhouse gave voice to the meaning of comradeship at home when she wrote in tribute to her husband,

> My debt to you, Beloved,
> Is one I cannot pay,
> In any coin of any realm
> On any reckoning day;
> For where is he shall figure
> The debt, when all is said,
> To one who makes you dream again
> When all the dreams were dead?
> Or where is the appraiser
> Who shall the claim compute,
> Of one who makes you sing again
> When all the songs were mute?[4]

We are blessed in our essential aloneness if we have found one who can make us sing again "When all the songs were mute."

There was, quite obviously, solitariness and loneliness in the experience of Jessie Rittenhouse. There were times when her "dreams were dead," and her song muted. Haunting depression is suggested in the lines she wrote, but in leaning her life upon another she found the grace and strength to sing again and to revive her dreams. Such is the book of caring companionship. We cannot live greatly without it.

It may be, too, that we cannot live greatly without the loneliness of valleys and shadows that temper our minds with understanding and insight. Perhaps songless days are the necessary prelude to inspiring music. Possibly dead dreams and the dust and ashes of broken hopes are the impetus to life's renewal. It is what happens in our solitude, what resources we bring to lonely valleys, that determines the issues of life. It is what we find in caring fellowship that revives our muted songs.

We need, you and I, both solitude in the company of minds that are an asset, and fellowship with those who care in order to make life meaningful and vital.

ILLUMINATING SOLITUDE

Commonly we prefer society to solitude. If we are of necessity alone, we compensate for the absence of comradeship with noise, with television, radio, or hi-fi, with anything to avoid lonely nothingness. All these, of course, have their place, but they are not an adequate substitute for solitude as a means to reflection. They are, for the most part, likely to be thought stoppers whose function is to enervate the mind.

Life, however, is altogether superficial if we have no time for ivory towers; time for thinking and the play of imagination. Our noblest aspirations and our finest hopes are born in solitude. Committee meetings seldom are creative, and the contemporary interest in "brain-storming" in groups is valuable only if members of the group have done their homework in solitude. The insights of our solitude may be sharpened and clarified in groups, but the seeds of thought are sowed in silence.

Only when we are alone are we able to sense the magic of our mysterious universe and capture something of its meaning. In quietness the saints and sages of the past whisper in our listening ears and we hear the "still small voice" of yesterday and the day before. In the brooding silence of our solitude we digest our own experience and discover the significance of pain and suffering, joy and peace.

Ralph Waldo Emerson once said that "The walls of the mind's chamber are covered with scribblings, which need but the bringing of a candle to render them intelligible." Our accumulated memories and experiences, our knowledge and our feelings have left scribblings on our minds to be deciphered in solitude. The scribblings, often only on the periphery of consciousness, contain a wealth of wisdom when they are brought to light and sorted in the silence. We cannot know the glories of the lighted mind except in quiet isolation from the hurrying crowds.

Wordsworth was no recluse, but he understood the necessity for solitude to illuminate the mind. He wrote,

> I am not One who much or oft delight
> To season my fireside with personal talk . . .

> Better than such discourse doth silence long,
> Long, barren silence square with my desire;
> To sit without emotion, hope, or aim,
> In the loved presence of my cottage-fire
> And listen to the flapping of the flame,
> Or kettle whispering its faint under-song.[5]

The "scribblings" Wordsworth brought to light from his fertile mind enriched the life of all mankind.

There are gems of insight in every mind waiting to emerge from the unconscious to illumine our lives and perhaps the lives of others. They are like buried treasure waiting to be found. Unhappily, in most of us they lie undiscovered beneath the clutter of trivia that occupy our days. We do too much and think too little. Florence Crowther notes of women that they "use their education to run washing machines, chauffeur the children and gather at the super-market, more for gossip than for gastronomy. From morning until time to thaw out their TV dinners, they are on the go, tending the appliances which have robbed them of their leisure, or subject to the tyranny of the telephone."

A friend of mine found what he called his "meditation room," both intellectually and spiritually rewarding. He said that often in the quiet he came to know what he had only half-known before. He searched the deeps of his mind for its hidden secrets and came away both enlightened and refreshed.

Quite possibly most of us cannot afford the luxury of a "meditation room," but we can cultivate the art of shutting out the world even in the tumult of a crowded city. A Chinese friend suggested he could close out the world anywhere by simply folding his hands, focusing his eyes upon them, and sitting quietly, looking neither to the right nor left. He said he could enjoy solitude even on a crowded street car and let his mind listen to the murmuring of the centuries. Perhaps I should say that his was a mind alive and full of quiet wisdom.

Another friend, whose responsibilities are vast in a great metropolitan area, who has served the government of the nation with distinction, and who is the president of a bank, told me he frequently has a luncheon date with himself. He finds a quiet corner table where he can avoid being seen by those who might recognize him, and there he spends his luncheon hour in meditation. The quality of the books he has written and the speeches he has given testify to the significance of his solitude. It is a solitude made possible by his own self-discipline.

In a letter, explaining why he did not marry, Nietzsche, the German philosopher, explained he could not afford the bondage of a wife and children and still preserve the vitality of his mind. "Better to live poor, sickly and aloof in some out-of-the-way corner," he wrote, "than to fill a pigeon hole in this modern world of mediocrity."[6] Nietzsche found aloneness intellectually rewarding and stimulating and he wrote magnificently. He carried his aloneness too far, however, and so missed the importance of love and fellowship to broaden the solitary mind.

We need solitude, you and I, to clarify the hidden hieroglyphics etched into our minds and to bring to birth the wisdom latent, but as yet undiscovered. Too much of society thwarts creative thinking. We need to be alone.

DISCIPLINED SOLITUDE

In our disciplined solitude we need to keep a cautious balance between looking inward and looking outward. The lonely brooding of the self over its failures and its hurts leaves us stricken with poverty of mind and spirit. It drives us to despair and into the depths of self-pity. Blaise Pascal, observing those who shared the places of the mighty, noted that "The king is surrounded by persons whose only thought is to divert the king. . . . For he is unhappy, king though he be, if he think of himself."[7]

There is a place, of course, for self-examination and we need to know ourselves. We need to examine the subtleties of our minds, the easy rationalizations by means of which we seek to deceive ourselves, the prejudices that distort our thinking, the emotions that betray our logic. We need to examine our opinions in the light of our interests and to see whether the truth we hold to be the truth is colored by our wishes. We are constrained to ascertain if "what goes without saying" is still going.

When life has gone askew and we are busy seeking scapegoats for our plight, one major question must be faced. It is the question each of the twelve disciples asked when Jesus said, "One of you will betray me." The question pained each one, "Master, is it I?" We wish we could avoid the question and normally we turn from it to preserve our pride. But there is neither healing nor help in avoiding painful questions. We do not find the way to life by avoiding the issues of the self.

The lonely pain of avoidance, leaving the agonizing questions about ourselves unanswered, is far different from the creative solitude that dares to see the self in all its somber colors and to fashion a nobler being from the wreckage of today. Surely Augustine would not have become St. Augustine if he had not finally faced himself. His *Confessions* bare his soul and mark a turning point of creative renewal.

Two men who came for counseling suggest the need for meditative self-appraisal. Both of them had lost their jobs. The fault was their own. One of them said, "My boss disliked me from the beginning." The other said, "I was a fool." Both of them had spent endless hours thinking about their problems. Only one of them asked the necessary question, "Master, is it I?" The one who asked the essential question is back at work and doing well. The other remains unemployed.

Our aloneness is only lonely pain and meaningless frustration when we play the part of evaders and refuse to examine ourselves. Solitude is creative if we come to grips with the follies and the faults within ourselves and think our way to life's renewal. We cannot change ourselves until we change our minds about ourselves.

There are times when a man's struggle with himself becomes creative. It was so in the life of St. Augustine when he confessed the fault within himself and began to see himself as a child of God for whom Christ died. The focus of his thought shifted from himself to God and he changed direction in the midstream of his life. If there were times when his struggle had overtones of protest, it was the tension between the actual and the unattained ideal that was creative. Perhaps he understood that

> When the fight begins within himself
> A man's worth something.[8]

And it is so.

The mind of Sören Kierkegaard was not at peace, and his writing was the articulation of his struggle to find himself and

God. Tolstoi, at war with the world and with himself, used his pen to relieve the tension in his soul. His solitude was tortured by the anguish of the world, and his creative power came from the tension. Both Kierkegaard and Tolstoi used their writing as a means to self-discovery and creative insight.

It is significant to note that neither Kierkegaard nor Tolstoi found peace of mind, but better yet they found strength of mind. What is more, they found wisdom both for themselves and others. If they did not attain serenity, at least they did not cease from struggle. Perhaps they were trouble-born stars whose light would guide succeeding generations of seekers.

THE HARVEST OF SOLITUDE

Happily, there are those whose solitude is free from tortured thoughts about the self. Their minds are free to roam the vast ocean of ideas, to touch the realms of beauty and goodness. Poets before Wordsworth had written greatly on great themes, but he was able to write of what had been ignored as commonplace and interpret the greatness of meaning hidden in it. He "saw things that other people do not see, and he saw with quite unique clearness and frequency things which they see at most rarely and dimly."[9]

The solitary vigils of Wordsworth had their issue in what he called "the harvest of the quiet eye." Henry Thoreau, isolated at Walden Pond, found doors of beauty and insight opening into his solitude. His description of "an owl . . . sitting on one of the lower dead limbs of a white pine . . . in broad daylight" is a marvel of descriptive genius wrought by quiet and unhurried observation. Watching the sleepy owl, annoyed by human intrusion, yet unable to remain alert, Thoreau noted, "I too felt a slumberous influence . . . he sat . . . with his eyes half open, like a cat."[10]

It was Mark Van Doren who said of Thoreau that "He craved for the sight and feel of facts." The facts he encountered as he exposed himself to the detail of things and place were inward events for him. Everything he touched led him to the threshold of discovery. The way the cat twitched his tail, the squirrel buried a nut, or the ice on the pond broke up in the spring were episodes that happened to him and in him with the freshness of a constant awakening.

Capacity to concentrate on ideas, things, and values awaits tranquility, which is nothing more than the good ordering of the mind. The mind that is saturated by its self-concern and disease is incapable of achieving "the harvest of the quiet eye." The great Cappadocian bishop of the fourth century, St. Basil, noted the barrier to creative solitude when he wrote to a friend: "I hesitate to write what I myself do in this solitude, night and day, seeing that although I have left the distractions of the city, which are to me the occasion of innumerable evils, I have not yet succeeded in forsaking myself."

Our capacity to feel and understand the events and simple facts around us that bring us to the threshold of discovery often is inhibited by the invasion of intruders from the self. Our concentration on the darting movements of the hummingbird are unknowingly interrupted by some inner yearning. The beauty and mystery of "sunset and evening sky" are distorted by some prodding disappointment. The wonder of a spreading spruce tree sheltering a robin's nest is lost in the clutches of a vagrant anxiety.

Nevertheless, the facts and the beauty, the events and the episodes that invite discovery and enrichment are there awaiting "the harvest of the quiet eye." They await the solitude that has ceased to be disturbed by the fussed, frantic, and fidgety intrusions of the self. They will enter then with gentle power to touch life with beauty and insight and we shall know, as Wordsworth did, that

> One impulse from a vernal wood
> May teach you more of man,
> Of moral evil and of good,
> Than all the sages can.[11]

BEYOND LONELINESS TO CREATIVE SOLITUDE

The great ideas and insights that have burst upon the world have come both from minds in tumult, struggling in lonely grandeur, and from minds free to roam in tranquil solitude. But in either case they have come from concentration. It was Max Bruch who noted that many a composer of great music has no choice but to conform to two laws, "solitude and concentration." He must be absolutely alone and undisturbed in his labors. As Wordsworth wrote,

> I must be, else sinning greatly,
> A dedicated spirit,[12]

committed unreservedly to the task at hand.

The future probably will affirm that Albert Einstein was the most creative scientific genius of our generation. A headline writer once headed a biographical review of Einstein's life with the words, "Splendid in Bitter Isolation." There are those who would question whether his isolation was "bitter," and yet it was costly in terms of family relations. There is something of the mood of Greek tragedy in the letter he wrote to his wife from Berlin suggesting she divorce him. "You will see that I will always remain true to you in my way," he wrote. Thereafter, he often went to Zurich to visit her and their two sons. During these interludes, Mileva, his wife, and the boys were keenly aware of Einstein's love for them. It was a heartfelt love. "While it was there it was very strong," the elder boy remembered. "He needed to be loved himself. But almost the instant you felt the contact, he would push you away. He would not let himself go. He would turn off his emotion like a tap."

No doubt his "turning off emotion like a tap" was Einstein's defense against intrusions into his dedicated quest for truth. His mind had to be totally committed to the signs and symbols of mathematics that in the end would reveal the secret of relativity and provide the formula to unlock the ultimate power of the physical universe. He was not unaware of the personal cost of his dedication. He wrote:

I have never belonged wholeheartedly to country or state, to my circle of friends, or even to my own family. Such isolation is sometimes bitter, but I do not regret being cut off from the understanding and sympathy of other men. I lose something by it, to be sure, but I am compensated for it in being rendered independent of the customs, opinions, and prejudices of others, and am not tempted to rest my peace of mind on such shifting foundations.[13]

Einstein carried his self-imposed aloneness to the limits of toleration.

The pursuits of the mind were Einstein's passion and his solitude was filled with his intellectual speculations. Alan W. Richards, a free-lance photographer, has described the Princeton years of the mathematical genius, who on one occasion tumbled into a manhole while walking preoccupied along Mercer Street at dusk. Careless of his personal appearance, Einstein usually dressed "in baggy pants and an old sweater." His mustache was "scraggly," and his hair looked "as if it hadn't been combed or cut for months." He was indifferent toward many of the normal concerns of everyday men.

Mr. Richards was struck by the fact that Einstein

automatically ignored the trivial, whether it happened to be a stranger's rudeness or a cut on the cheek. He simplified his concerns in order to spend his brain wisely.[14]

It would be fair to say, I think, that Einstein's life was uncluttered. He was in no sense arrogant. On the contrary, deep humility pervaded all he said and did. He spoke only with unaffected kindness and with respect for everyone, child or adult. He could not remember names. They seemed superfluous to a mind filled with an orderly file of mathematical symbols which he never forgot.

The tranquil solitude of Einstein is far beyond the capacity of most of us. We cannot turn off our emotions "like a tap" even when we wish we could do so. We are involved with those we love and we wish to give ourselves to them, not to push them away. We do care how we appear to others and the trivia of combed hair and pressed trousers are significant trivia. Perhaps genius can afford to ignore the normal niceties of human appearance, but most of us do not qualify as geniuses.

It should be observed, however, that there are times when fruitful solitude requires a concentration bypassing emotions that distort our thought. Random annoyances and remembered conflicts distort the mind's clarity. Feelings fling their fetters around the brain and squeeze its arteries dry. It is only in dedicated concentration, eliminating the extraneous, that the mind flows free and finds itself creative.

That is not to say there is not passion in our thinking. Einstein felt his formula and there was a glowing emotional tone that enveloped his mind in thought. The poet feels as he thinks and his words carry emotional conviction, but his feelings are not random, they are channeled and directed like "a strong, steady wind, that blows one way." The musician feels as he thinks, and the notes he puts on paper are more than mechanical. Nevertheless, his emotions and his thoughts move together in the same direction. There are unwanted emotions that he "turns off like a tap," simply because he must.

We move necessarily from involvement to isolation, from the concerns of comradeship, to aloneness. Our involvement in the lives of others requires a certain care for trivia, trivia of dress and personal grooming that become automatic and not a consuming passion. At the same time, the trivia are crowded from our minds in times of thoughtful solitude. In short, creative minds are disciplined to deal with one thing at a time in an ordered sequence, not a cluttered confusion.

It should be noted, too, that creative solitude requires humility of mind. The genuine humility of Einstein made a lasting impression on all who shared his life and thought. There was no arrogance in his genius, no ego protruding through the symbols of his craft. He respected other minds and was open to the insights of the lesser minds he plucked. He was no solitary egoist, flaunting his opinions and retreating in disdain from criticism.

Maurice H. Small, who studied the biographies and autobiographies of some one hundred recluses concluded that barely a dozen of them suffered lonely neglect because they entertained ideas too advanced for their generations. Most of them were arrogant, assuming their opinions were the final word. Small went on to insist there are two general types of solitary egoists. There are those who are intensely subjective, retreating from fellowship because they feel powerless to compete with the minds and the capacities of others. Then, there are the self-asserting and self-approving who resent the refusal of society to respond to their efforts with unqualified approval.

There are others, however, whose solitude is humble, open-minded, and noncombative. They seek the truth that is the road to freedom and they have no pride of opinion. Alan Richards says of Einstein's Theory of Relativity that

it seems to have come—from more than mere brilliance—from a combination of humility and imaginative daring. Perhaps the very act of making his discoveries about matter stirred him with both a sense of wonder at what the human brain could perceive, and a feeling of insignificance from realizing how small a part man plays in the vast logic of the universe. When I asked Dean Ernest Gordon of the Princeton University chapel how he would explain Einstein's great intellect with great simplicity, he said, "I think it was his sense of reverence."[15]

The words of Dean Gordon bring us to the essence of creative solitude, namely, "the sense of reverence." The wise man in his solitariness contemplates the world of things and ideas, the universe of earth and sky, land and seas, space and time with reverent awe and humility. His egotism is destroyed by his feeling of insignificance in the presence of the mysterious universe. To him, "The heavens declare the glory of God and the firmament showeth his handiwork."

So it is that in humility we wait in the solitude for whatever revelations are vouchsafed to our minds. If the vision tarries, we wait for it in confidence that it will come. As Schopenhauer said long ago, a picture should be looked at as a royal person approached, in silence, until the moment it pleases him to speak. If we speak first, we expose ourselves to hear nothing but the sound of our own voices. So, if we are wise, we wait in reverence and awe for the authentic voice of reality and truth to make our silences fruitful and to take us beyond loneliness to creative solitude.

Notes

Introduction

1. Emily Dickinson, "Beclouded." Reprinted by permission of the publishers and trustees of Amherst College, from Thomas H. Johnson, editor, *The Poems of Emily Dickinson* (Cambridge, Mass: The Belknap Press of Harvard University Press), p. 760. Copyright 1951, 1955 by the President and Fellows of Harvard College.

CHAPTER 1. *Lonely Landscape*

1. Amy Lowell, "The Day That Was That Day," in *Selected Poems* (Boston: Houghton Mifflin, 1928), p. 146. Reprinted by permission of the publisher.
2. Samuel Coleridge, "The Rime of the Ancient Mariner," pt. IV, st. iii.
3. Alfred Tennyson, "In Memoriam," pt. LV, st. ii.
4. Walter Prescott Webb, *The Great Plains* (Boston: Ginn & Co., 1931), p. 488.
5. Edna St. Vincent Millay, *Collected Poems* (New York: Harper, 1956), pp. 548–9.
6. Rudyard Kipling, "The Stranger." *Rudyard Kipling's Verse* (New York: Doubleday-Page & Co., 1926), p. 616.
7. Mary McDermott Shideler, "We Saw You a Stranger," in *The Christian Century,* LXXXI (Dec. 23, 1964), p. 1585.
8. Theodor Reik, *Voices from the Inaudible* (New York: Farrar, Straus, 1964), p. 123.
9. Howard Spring, *Flame Is the Spur.* Quoted from William Hordern, *A Layman's Guide to Protestant Theology* (New York: Macmillan, 1955), pp. 101–2.
10. Robert Ardrey, *Sing Me No Lullaby.* Quoted from review by Brooks Atkinson in *The New York Times,* Oct. 24, 1954.

CHAPTER 2. *Lonely Inscape*

1. Robert Frost, "Desert Places," in *Complete Poems of Robert Frost* (New York: Holt, Rinehart and Winston, 1962), p. 386. Reprinted by permission of the publisher.

2. Edward Dyer, *"My Mind to Me a Kingdom Is,"* in *Harvard Classics,* XL (New York: Collier, 1910), p. 211.

3. Elizabeth Spencer, *Knights and Dragons* (New York: McGraw-Hill, 1965), p. 168.

4. John 16:32.

5. William H. Miller, Press Release from the American Oil Co., June 3, 1965.

6. Matt. 7:14.

7. Walt Whitman, "Song of Myself," in *Leaves of Grass* (New York: The Heritage Press, 1949), p. 25.

8. Author unknown.

9. Walt Whitman, "Crossing Brooklyn Ferry," in *Leaves of Grass* (New York: The Heritage Press, 1949), p. 43.

10. Luke 18:13.

11. Sinclair Lewis, *Babbitt* (New York: Harcourt, Brace, 1950), p. 401.

12. T. S. Eliot, "The Love Song of J. Alfred Prufrock," in *The Complete Poems and Plays* (New York: Harcourt, Brace, 1952), p. 5. Reprinted by permission of the publisher.

13. Mark 4:28.

14. Petrarch, *The Life of Solitude,* tr. by Jacob Zeitlin, (Urbana, Ill.: University of Illinois Press, 1924), p. 171.

15. Letter to the author's wife.

16. Karl Augustus Menninger, *The Vital Balance* (New York: Viking, 1963), pp. 391–2.

17. Heb. 11:1.

18. John 6:21.

CHAPTER 3. *We All Need Each Other*

1. Eccles. 4:9–10.

2. Deut. 4:10–11.

3. Alfred Tennyson, "Ulysses," in *Poetical Works* (Boston: Noughton, Osgood, 1879), p. 56.

4. Henry W. Longfellow, "The Theologian's Tale, Elizabeth," in *Tales of a Wayside Inn,* III, iv.

5. Matt. 5:23–4.

6. Deut. 5:17.

7. Matt. 5:22.

8. *Ibid.*

9. Violet Alleyn Story, "Prayer in Affliction," from *Masterpieces of Religious Verse,* James Dalton Morrison, ed., (New York: Harper & Row), 1948, p. 1452.

10. Matt. 5:24.

11. Matt. 6:12.

12. Newlan Fowler, *Franz Schubert and His Circle* (New York: Tudor, 1935), p. 167.
13. Don M. Wolfe, *The Image of Man in America* (Dallas: Southern Methodist University Press, 1957), pp. 417–8.
14. Dwight D. Eisenhower, *Crusade in Europe* (New York: Doubleday, 1948), p. 472.
15. Aldous Huxley, *Tomorrow and Tomorrow and Tomorrow and Other Essays* (New York: Harper, 1956), p. 68.
16. Mark Schorer, *Sinclair Lewis: An American Life* (New York: Mc-Graw-Hill, 1961), p. 792.
17. Theodor Reik, *Voices from the Inaudible* (New York: Farrar, Straus, 1964), p. 188.
18. Matt. 4:4.
19. Theodor Reik, *Voices from the Inaudible* (New York: Farrar, Straus, 1964), pp. 106–7.
20. John 15:12.
21. Richard Crowder, *Carl Sandburg* (New York: Twayne, 1964), p. 99.

CHAPTER 4. *Strange Estrangement*

1. Ps. 68:6.
2. T. S. Eliot, *The Cocktail Party* (New York: Harcourt, Brace, 1950), p. 98. Reprinted by permission of the publisher.
3. Lenore Marshall, *Other Knowledge: Poems, New and Selected* (New York: Noonday Press), p. 6. Copyright © 1956 by Lenore G. Marshall. Reprinted by permission of the publisher.
4. Morris L. West, *The Shoes of the Fisherman* (New York: William Morrow, 1963), pp. 92–3.
5. Mark 8:36.
6. Jean Ingelow. Quoted from J. Wallace Hamilton, *Horns and Halos in Human Nature* (Westwood, N.J.: Revell, 1954), p. 144.
7. Thomas Wolfe, *You Can't Go Home Again* (New York: Harper, 1940), p. 56.
8. Robert Penn Warren, *The Cave* (New York: Random House, 1959). Quoted from review by Arthur Mizener in *The New York Times,* Aug. 23, 1959.
9. Alfred Tennyson, from "The Passing of Arthur," in "Idylls of the King."

CHAPTER 5. *Countdown Alone*

1. Edwin Markham, "Man Test," in *Poems of Edwin Markham* (New York: Harper, 1950), p. 6.
2. Joel 3:14.
3. Thomas Babbington Macaulay, "Lord Clive," in *Critical and Historical Essays* (New York: Albert Mason, 1875), pp. 46–47.

4. Regina Westcott Wieman, *What the American Family Faces* (Chicago: Eugene Hugh, 1943), pp. 15–6.
5. Arthur Koestler, *Darkness at Noon* (New York: Modern Library, 1941), pp. 43–4.
6. Arthur S. Link, *Wilson: Road to the White House* (Princeton: Princeton University Press, 1947), pp. 371–2.
7. W. B. Yeats, "The Second Coming," in *Collected Poems* (New York: Macmillan, 1940), p. 215. Copyright 1924 by the Macmillan Company. Copyright renewed 1952 by Bertha Georgia Yeats. Reprinted by permission of the publisher.
8. J. B. Phillips, *Good News* (New York: Macmillan, 1963), pp. 33–4.
9. Archibald MacLeish, from "Variations on an Undiscovered Theme, in honor of both Judge Augustus N. Hand, and his son, the Honorable Learned Hand."
10. Prov. 22:28.
11. John Baillie, *The Sense of the Presence of God* (New York: Scribner, 1962), p. 143.
12. K. C. Wu, *The Lane of Eternal Stability* (New York: Crown, 1962), pp. 212–3.
13. *Ibid.*

CHAPTER 6. *Guilty Outsider*

1. Axel Munthe, *The Story of San Michele* (London: J. Murray, 1929), p. 46.
2. Gen. 4:13.
3. O. Hobart Mowrer, *New Group Therapy* (Princeton: Van Nostrand, 1964), p. 27.
4. *Ibid.*
5. William Shakespeare, *Hamlet,* III, iii.
6. *Ibid.*
7. Eugene O'Neill, *The Iceman Cometh* (New York: Vintage, 1956), p. 238.
8. William Wordsworth, *The Complete Poetical Works of William Wordsworth* (Boston: Houghton Mifflin, 1932), p. 296.
9. Ps. 19:12.
10. I John 1:8.
11. Van Wyck Brooks, *The Confident Years* (New York: Dutton, 1952), p. 236.
12. II Tim. 2:15 (AV).
13. *The Wall Street Journal,* Editorial.
14. Sloan Wilson, *Man in the Gray Flannel Suit* (New York: Simon and Schuster, 1955), pp. 262–3.
15. T. S. Eliot, *The Cocktail Party* (New York: Harcourt, Brace, 1950), p. 186. Reprinted by permission of the publisher.

16. Katherine Anthony, *The Lambs* (New York: Alfred A. Knopf, 1945), p. 104.
17. I John 1:9.
18. Augustus M. Toplady, "Rock of Ages," st. viii.

CHAPTER 7. *I'm Sorry for Me*

1. Vardis Fisher, *Thomas Wolfe as I Knew Him and Other Essays* (Denver: Alan Swallow, 1963), p. 34.
2. Chicago *Tribune,* July 24, 1963.
3. Quoted from Seward Hiltner, *Self-Understanding through Psychology and Religion* (New York: Scribner, 1951), p. 56.
4. Samuel Smith, "The Morning Light Is Breaking."
5. A. E. Housman, *Collected Poems* (New York: Holt, Rinehart and Winston, 1959), p. 110.
6. Gen. 32:24.
7. II Cor. 4:8.
8. Ps. 31:9.
9. Ps. 31:23–4.
10. Ps. 31:9.
11. Hab. 2:3.
12. A. E. Housman, "Epitaph on an Army of Mercenaries," in *Collected Poems* (New York: Holt, Rinehart and Winston, 1959), p. 110. Reprinted by permission of the publisher.
13. Nevil Shute, *Pastoral* (New York: William Morrow, 1944), pp. 133–4.
14. Ps. 84:6.
15. Robert Browning, "Rabbi Ben Ezra," st. vi.
16. Heb. 12:2.
17. Ps. 84:6.
18. Job 3:23.
19. Job 38:4; 6.
20. Job 13:15.

CHAPTER 8. *Isolated by Illness*

1. Leonard Kriegel, *The Long Walk Home* (New York: Appleton-Century, 1964), p. 33.
2. Lin Yu-tang, *The Importance of Living* (New York: Day, Reynal and Hitchcock, 1937), pp. 29–30.
3. David Grayson, *Adventures in Solitude* (Garden City: Doubleday, Doran, 1931), pp. 4–5.
4. Peter Bowman, *Beach Red* (New York: Random House, 1945), p. 3.
5. Exod. 15:2.
6. II Cor. 12:9.
7. Ps. 119:67.
8. Ps. 119:68.

9. Ps. 119:66.
10. Heb. 5:8.
11. Isa. 53:5.
12. Isa. 53:7.
13. Isa. 53:5.
14. II Cor. 12:9.

CHAPTER 9. *Give Me Your Tears*

1. Quoted from Doremus, *The Heights of Christian Blessedness* (New York: Abingdon,), p. 34.
2. Lam. 2:18.
3. John 21:17.
4. *See* Seward Hiltner, *Self-Understanding through Psychology and Religion* (New York: Scribner, 1951), pp. 180–2.
5. Alfred Tennyson, "In Memoriam," pt. XXVII, st. iv.
6. Job 2:11.
7. Job 42:5.
8. Jewish hymn, "Why Art Thou Cast Down."
9. Edwin Markham, "Your Tears," in *Poems of Edwin Markham* (New York: Harper, 1950), p. 141.
10. Matt. 28:20.
11. I Cor. 1:23.
12. Alfred Tennyson, "In Memoriam," pt. LIV.
13. Ps. 23.4.

CHAPTER 10. *Creative Solitude*

1. John Milton, *Paradise Lost*, VIII, pp. 363–5.
2. William Cowper, "The Solitude of Alexander Selkirk," in *Harvard Classics*, XLI (New York: Collier, 1910), p. 548.
3. Henry W. Longfellow, "The Theologian's Tale, Elizabeth," in *Tales of a Wayside Inn*, III, iv.
4. Jessie B. Rittenhouse, "Debt," from *Door of Dreams* (Boston: Houghton Mifflin Co., 1918), p. 3. Reprinted by permission of the publisher.
5. William Wordsworth, "Personal Talk," Sonnet 1.
6. Forster Nietzsche, *The Lonely Nietzsche* (London: William Heineman, 1965), pp. 315–6.
7. Blaise Pascal, *Misery of Man Without God*, in *Harvard Classics*, XLVII (New York: Collier, 1910), p. 53.
8. Robert Browning, "Bishop Bloughram's Apology."
9. H. W. Garrod, *Wordsworth: Lectures and Essays* (Oxford: Clarendon Press, 1923), p. 95.
10. Henry D. Thoreau, *Walden* (Mount Vernon: Peter Pauper Press, n.d.), pp. 257–8.

11. William Wordsworth, "Lines Written in Early Spring," st. vi.

12. William Wordsworth, *The Complete Poetical Works of William Wordsworth* (Boston: Houghton Mifflin, 1932), p. 83.

13. Peter Michelmore, *Einstein: Profile of the Man* (New York: Dodd, Mead, 1965). Quoted from review by William L. Laurence in *The New York Times,* Nov. 25, 1962.

14. Alan Richards, Trenton, New Jersey *Times,* March 14, 1962.

15. *Ibid.*

Index

Addams, Jane   58
anger   38, 39, 40–43, 55, 114
Anthony, Katherine   93
anxiety   14–16, 22, 33, 91, 94, 103, 122, 124
Ardrey, Robert   15
August, Karl   132

Bacon, Francis   147
Baillie, John   80
Barth, Karl   79, 142
Berry, Charles Francis   71
Bismarck   40
Bonaparte, Napoleon   79
Bowman, Peter   120
Bradley, J. Chapman   16
Brooks, Van Wyck   89
Browning, Robert   107, 132, 154
Bruch, Max   157
Buddha   137
Bunyan, John   56
Byrd, Admiral   126
Byron, Lord   128

Cain   83
Carlyle, Thomas   133
Chastain, Madye Lee   106
Choguill, Orlo   106
choice   68–75, 79–81, 86, 146
Churchill, Winston   105
Ciardi, John   14
Cicero   149
Clive, Lord   69

Coleridge, Samuel   4
Columbus, Christopher   35
commitment   23, 25, 27, 30, 97
communication   1–5, 12, 13, 34, 47, 52, 57–58, 63 99
connectedness   3, 13, 17
Cousins, Norman   15
Cowper, William   146, 149
Cromwell, Oliver   70
Crowther, Florence   152

Dante   134
Da Vinci, Leonardo   74
Dennis the Menace   89
Deuteronomy   35
Dickinson, Emily   vii
disconnectedness   2, 12, 13, 15
Doremus   134
Doren, Mark van   155
Dyer, Edward   19

Ecclesiastes   34
Edison, Thomas   20
Einstein, Albert   157–160
Eisenhower, Dwight   47
Elijah   99–100
Eliot, T. S.   29, 53, 93
Emerson, Ralph Waldo   79, 130, 151

Fischer, Vardis   101
forgiveness   95 ff.
Fox, George   124

Frankl, Viktor   14
Freud, Sigmund   55, 95
Frost, Robert   18

Gary, Raymond   73
Gibbon, Edward   113
Goethe, Johann Wolfgang von   112, 132
Gordon, Dean   160
Grayson, David   114–115, 119
grief   8, 9 ff., 132 ff.
Gunther, John   76–77, 127

Hand, Augustus N.   78
Handel, George Fredrich   112
Harding, Warren   15
Hardy, Thomas   104
Hebrews   79, 113, 128
Hell   38, 53
Herford, Brooke   72
Hiltner, Seward   140
hostilities   7, 25, 36–39, 42–45
hostility   7, 13, 26, 33, 37–45
Housman, A. E.   104, 111
Hügel, Baron von   125
Hughes, Langston   12
Huxley, Aldous   4, 47

Ingelow, Jean   60
ingratitude   76–77
inscape   viii, 17–22, 24–29, 33, 82
Isaiah   112, 129

Jacob   104, 136
Jesus   23, 29, 33, 37–38, 43, 45, 49, 56, 70, 79, 84, 86, 113, 115, 126, 128, 135, 141, 153–154
Jezebel   99
Job   114, 139–140
Joel   67
I John   87
Johnson, Samuel   69
Jung, Carl   102

Kant, Immanuel   5
Keats, John   19, 130
King, Martin Luther   41
Kipling, Rudyard   9

Kirkegaard, Sören   154–155
Koestler, Arthur   74
Kollwitz, Käethe   138
Kriegel, Leonard   117

Lamb, Charles   12, 93–94
Lamb, Mary   93–94
Lawrence, Marjorie   125
Lee, Robert E.   75
Lewis, Sinclair   28, 42, 48
Lincoln, Abraham   50
Lindemann, Erich   136
Lippmann, Walter   14
Locke, John   36
London, Jack   88–89
Longfellow, Henry Wadsworth   4
Lowell, Amy   1
Lowell, James Russell   149

Macaulay, Thomas B.   69
MacLeish, Archibald   13, 14, 24, 78
Mamchur, Stephen   55
Mansfield, Katherine   130, 132
Markham, Edwin   67, 142
Marshall, Catherine   124
Marshall, Lenore G.   53
Marty, Martin   73
Marx, Karl   42
Matheson, George   131
Melville, Herman   69
Menninger, Karl Augustus   30
Millay, Edna St. Vincent   8, 104
Miller, William H.   23
Milton, John   19, 112, 126, 145, 148
Morley, Christopher   18
Mowrer, O. Hobart   84
Munthe, Axel   82
Murry, J. Middleton   132

Naaman   75
Nadeau, Remi   12, 13
Nelson, Lord   71
Newsweek   54
Newton, Isaac   143
New York *World*   76
Niebuhr, Reinhold   88
Nietzsche, Friedrich Wilhelm   83, 153

Oda, Makuto   74
O. Henry   85
Olsen, Tillie   135, 140
Olson, Karl   2
O'Neill, Eugene   86
Overstreet, Harry   43

Pascal, Blaise   153
Pasternak, Boris   16
Peterson, Houston   68
Petrarch   30
Phillips, J. B.   78
Pickering, Thomas   142
Pope, Alexander   130
prayer   31, 84, 124, 141
Proverbs   79
Pyle, Ernie   104–105

Reik, Theodor   48
Richards, Alan W.   158, 160
Rittenhouse, Jessie   150

St. Augustine   84, 86, 154
St. Basil   156
St. John   49
St. Luke   120
St. Paul   21, 27, 40, 76, 98, 107,
    120, 127, 131
St. Peter   135
Sampson, Anthony   77
Sandburg, Carl   32, 50, 147
Sartre, Jean-Paul   3, 24, 86
Saturday Review   58
Scherer, Paul   130
Schopenhauer, Arthur   160
Schorer, Mark   48
Schriner, Al   102
Schubert, Franz   46
Schurz, Carl   42
Schweitzer, Albert   110
Scott, Sir Walter   128
self-acceptance   25
self-doubt   7
self-fulfillment   21, 23
self-hate   24, 42, 43, 86
self-pity   19–22, 99, 100 ff., 110,
    114, 139, 148, 149, 153
self-respect   27

Shakespeare, William   19, 68, 84
Shideler, Mary McDermott   10
Shute, Nevil   112
Small, Maurice H.   159
Smith, Samuel   103
Smuts, Jan   29
Spencer, Elizabeth   21
Spring, Howard   15
Stevenson, Adlai   54
Stevenson, Robert Louis   130–131
Story, Violet Alleyn   43
stranger   7, 9–12

Taubman, Howard   111
technology   4, 5, 17
Temple, Archbishop   72
Tennyson, Alfred   6, 36, 64–65,
    130, 138, 143–144
Thackeray, William M.   106
Thoreau, Henry   145, 155
Tillich, Paul   33
Timothy   76
Tolstoi, Leo   155
Toscanini, Arturo   97, 111
Twain, Mark   42

Ulysses   36

Veblen, Thorstein   4
Vergil   134

Wall Street Journal   90
Warren, Robert Penn   61
Weatherhead, Leslie   82
Webb, Walter Prescott   6–7
Webster, Noah   113
Wedel, Cynthia Clark   92
Weill, Kurt   12
West, Morris L.   55
Westberg, Granger   134
Whitman, Walt   25, 26, 142
Wieman, Henry N.   29, 73
Wieman, Regina   71
Wilson, Sloan   91
Wilson, Woodrow   76–77
Wilkiewisz, Stanislaw   109
Wolfe, Thomas   60

Wootton, Barbara 77

Wordsworth, William 19, 87, 151–
152, 155–157

Wu, K. C. 16, 80

Yeats, W. B. 77

Yutang, Lin 19